MW01671072

THE RED DOOR

AN HISTORICAL MEMOIR OF THE SQUIRREL HILL CAFE

Jan Cavrak & Leslie Anne Mcilroy

The Red Door

An Historical Memoir of The Squirrel Hill Cafe

by Jan Cavrak & Leslie Anne Mcilroy

Main Street Rag Publishing Company
Charlotte, North Carolina

Copyright © 2020 Main Street Rag Publishing Company
Cover painting by Kitty Correal, all rights reserved
Cover design by M. Scott Douglass
Photos by Amy Halle (unless otherwise noted), all rights reserved.

Library of Congress Control Number: 2020946020

ISBN: 978-1-59948-838-7

Produced in the United States of America

Main Street Rag Publishing Company
PO Box 690100
Charlotte, NC 28227
www.MainStreetRag.com

Acknowledgments:

For nearly three years, we have worked on putting this collection together, and we could not have done it alone. It is a book of stories that tells a larger one, which could not have been written without the shared experience, truth-telling and enthusiasm of the beloved Cage Crew and customers across the board—many who submitted their Cage memories for inclusion.

Thanks to the Nieri & McIntosh families, who generously shared all of their family history to trace back the beginning of The Squirrel Hill Cafe to 1916 when it opened as a fruit stand: Walt & Jack Nieri, John McIntosh, Jerry Gianni & Geraldine "Mac" McGartland.

Thanks to Helen Wilson from the Squirrel Hill Historical Society for helping us weasel out some pictures.

Thanks to Patty & Rod for opening their doors to our adventure, to Amy Halle for photos (please note that a few of the most sentient photos are of low quality; we apologize, but felt it pertinent to include them anyway). Thanks to Jeanne Scardamalia for assisting in research, to Silas Switzer for endless transcribing, to Kitty Correal for a stunning cover and to each and every one of you who make up The Cage Community—customers and crew—past and present!

See, you actually CAN go home again!

Love,
Jan Cavrak & Leslie Anne Mcilroy

PS: All permissions have been granted for use of photos and text included. No one has been compensated for their contributions.

Kitty Correal, artist, *The Red Door*

Preface
The Red Door—An Historical Memoir of The Squirrel Hill Cafe

The Red Door is not just a memoir, although it is told primarily through the eyes of Jan Cavrak, who has worked at Pittsburgh's historic Squirrel Hill Cafe (affectionately known as The Cage) for nearly 40 years. It is an exploration of what transforms a public space into a tangible community. It ponders the oeuvre—what collectively makes a space a destination—why people from all walks of life converge under a roof to celebrate the small ways they can be comforted, celebrated, challenged, voiced and heard. For years …

The book shares personal memories from patrons and personnel alike, across the spectrum: friendship and anger, marriage and divorce, love and longing, hunger and humor, homeless and home, especially home. If anything comes through the work of capturing individual moments and experiences at The Squirrel Hill Cafe, it is the clichéd notion of a "home away from home," a safe and welcoming place.

Regulars, "newbies," residents and passers-by all gather every day of the week—planned or unplanned—to affirm a necessary sense of belonging. No judgment, no motives, no need to engage or disengage. A diverse community of Pittsburghers who share The Cage as their common denominator.

The book was written over three years of intimate collaboration between two Pittsburgh natives, Jan Cavrak and writer Leslie Anne Mcilroy, who bartended at The Cage for almost 10 years in the 1980s/90s. It contains a wealth of photographs that help bring the reader into the ambiance and multeity of The Cage experience, including name-droppable contributors like novelist Stuart O'Nan, reporter Eric Heyl, producer Minette Seate and a tribute to the missed and memorialized Anthony Bourdain, who visited The Cage a year before he passed to film his Pittsburgh version of *Parts Unknown*.

Which brings us to the food (kind of)—a menu that has long served the Pittsburgh community well: burgers and hot balls, fries and chicken wings, the historic omelets and, Lord knows, the sardines and hard-boiled eggs, all a decadent spread; the flavors of history and hallowedness that satisfy the hunger of The Cage appetite.

Most remarkable, the book is the first to uncover the legacy of The Cage, complete with family interviews, photos, clippings and blueprints—a must for any historical bar buff!

Finally, we invite you into an unsolicited chapter of testimonials ("A Page in the Cage"): first-hand accounts of everything from fights and fervor, workings and shortcomings, day-to-day struggles, conflicts, people (beautiful and bastard), all the making of an iconic Pittsburgh institution that continues to thrive. How? Because, according to Jan, what really makes The Cage The Cage, is everyone who walks through The Red Door. A community of lovers and seekers, losers and dreamers, doers and decadents. Welcome home!

Squirrel Hill Cafe by Pittsburgh artist Michel Demetria Tsouris

The Red Door, 1981

It was May 1980. The 61A came to a stop at Forbes and Murray Avenues, home at the time to the nostalgic Gulf gas station and the famous Waldorf Bakery in Squirrel Hill.

"I crossed Murray Avenue and I seen a solid building, black and red with windows that looked like a tic-tac-toe board with 'The Squirrel Hill Cafe' and a couple of squirrels in red at the top," says Jan. "It didn't look like a Cafe with deli sandwiches and tea and stuff, but it did look like a cage. In the window, a 'Help Wanted' sign was scotch-taped to the glass. Written in black magic marker was 'Daytime waitress, 11 a.m. to 7 p.m. Inquire within.' I had waitressed some before. Couldn't hurt to try. I put my hand on the brass bar and pushed open the door, the red door, for the first time …

> *"What makes this room? Everyone who walks through that door."*
>
> **—Jan Cavrak**

"It was dark and cool—comforting. Just as you walk in was a ratty bulletin board with tattered posters advertising everything

from the Frick House and local bands to yard sales and lost pets.

I walked up the small ramp into a large room with a really high tin ceiling, tall, high-backed wooden booths on my right and regular tables in the middle. The bar was old—old and lived in—with a big round mirror and shelves and shelves of liquor beneath. It hadn't been cleaned in years, but I could see my reflection.

"In the far back were bathrooms, a pinball machine and a jukebox. I realized this wasn't the first time I had been here. When I was little, my dad brought me to Squirrel Hill to buy shoes at Little's; it was a big deal back then.

"One shoe day he brought me to The Cage. It wasn't illegal to bring a kid in then—people smoking and drinking were just a part of life. I remember sitting next to the jukebox looking at the mist from the steam table, never dreaming I would work here, and for so long. I noticed the dumbwaiter; I had no idea what it was or what it meant. Ends up, it goes up and

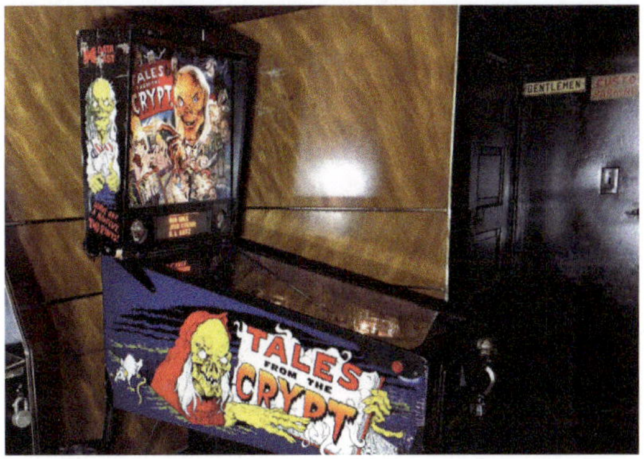

down to the cellar. It demands strength and luck. You have pull it by hand and back muscle, hauling up cases of beer, buckets of ice, a replacement for the empty bottle of Jacquin's.

"If you pull too fast, the rope slips off the wheel and it takes one to two men (I am a small woman) to set it straight. If you're busy, it's a nightmare. If not, you work it out—ask a couple of regulars to help.

"To the right of the bar are coolers for the 'fancy' bottled beers. Then, the prep table filled every morning from a hose in the kitchen—hot water to keep the food warm. Ronnie DeLallo, my soon-to-be boss, came in at six a.m. sharp. He made everything from scratch.

"I was kind of taking it all in for a bit longer than this feels written down when Ronnie came out of the kitchen sweating with a smoke in his mouth. He was short and balding and very Italian with gray hair; his eyebrow raised in a question. He was gruff, but friendly and wiped his hands on his apron before he introduced himself and shook mine.

"I don't know exactly how or why and I don't remember having a resume or anything, but Ronnie hired me on the spot. Actually, his brother John hired me. They had some kind of intuition—Italian.

"My strongest memory of my first day/ week was this: I went into the kitchen to

get pickles. They were in a glass gallon jug. It slipped out of my hands and smashed to the ground: shattered glass and dills everywhere. And, the smell! Ronnie just shook his head and Freddie, the prep cook, cleaned up my mess. Thank God for Freddie. I was embarrassed and grateful.

"One time we had a skunk behind the bar. This waitress, who was in training, came out of the cellar and face to face with the skunk that had a six-pack wrapper around its neck. Animal control came and took care of the poor thing, but Freddie was left with the smell. He tried everything to get the stench out of the kitchen: tomato juice, vinegar, everything. In the end, it was just time.

Freddie & Jan's grandson, Nicholas, who is now 24

"Freddie was a tiny man. He cleaned the bar in the morning and dishes over lunch. I wish I could remember what he drank. I think it was whiskey, some kind of whiskey. He hung out with John Gardner, a regular who came in every day. There used to be a picture behind the bar of the two of them. It is long gone, as is Freddie, who died.

"When Freddie's apartment burned down in the years he was working at The Cage, I remember Ronnie put a jar out for donations. That's the way Ronnie was. He wouldn't ask for anything for himself, but he would for others.

"Freddie was there for a few years. He used to call me 'kitty cat.' I am not sure why, but I liked it. Sometimes he would stand by the kitchen and take it all in as if he knew something we didn't. Freddie was a Cage fixture and then he was gone, like so many others .... "

For the past 12 years on our lunch hour, The Cage has been one of our regular stops, whether for their delicious burgers, hearty salads or even a simple grilled cheese sandwich. During these 12 years, the only constant has been our waitress Jan. We have seen her go from dark hair to her now gray do! Perhaps we have changed, too :-) She has always been kind and gave it to us straight when they didn't have what we wanted to eat that day, but we still remained. We don't have a story per se, but just like some of the other regulars that sit at the bar, we've become part of the story of The Cage.

—Dr. Edward J Horan, DMD Staff, Diane, Melinda & Denise

"I waitressed daylight for a few years while Big John and Bobby worked the bar. Some days were good, some bad. I learned to wear comfy shoes and to kind of put blinders on—a mental wall. That don't mean that I didn't have fun talking to my customers, just that you kind of have to have your guard up so you don't get mad or your feelings don't get hurt.

"Back then, my best friend Sandy (we have been friends for 55 years; she is my #1 co-pilot on road-trips), anyway, she worked at Carnegie Mellon University (CMU). She kept bugging me to come learn how to use a computer and work with her. But I had no desire. To this day I don't own a computer. I chose and still choose the bar. I've realized that though it drives me insane sometimes, it's also what keeps me from going crazy. I like the routine as much as the surprises.

"Also, during that time, I had been going to Nags Head with my dad for a week every year. We'd go in September when things were quiet. Those were the best three weeks of my year. We would hang out on the beach, visit the lighthouses and gift shops, and go to dinner. He'd pay and I'd tip."

"The last year, before he died, we went to this place called the Weeping Radish. The hostess tried to seat us in a dark back corner like we were lovers. 'He's not my sugar daddy,' I thought. 'He's my father.' We insisted on a new table, but laughed about it all of the time.

"After my father died, Ronnie put me behind the bar. He said he thought a change of scenery would do me good. He was right. I had never really bartended before, but he trusted me, so I just kind of fell into it. It was my Dad's death that marked the beginning of my career as a bartender at The Cage.

"Over the years, I guess I have developed a routine; I like routine. I get there every morning at 6 a.m. (although Patty says I don't have to be there until 9—I know) Wednesday through Saturday. I like getting there first, because I am an early bird by nature and because Squirrel Hill is empty and I can park where I want. Some mornings I am the only car on Forbes.

"On my way to the bar, I stop at the CVS to pick up a copy of the *Pittsburgh Post-Gazette* and say hi to Jason or Lee, who wait on me. Then I open the bar: I get the bar set up with ashtrays, lemons, limes, olives. Then I set the tables. But they have to be a certain way: ketchup, salt, pepper, sugar, ashtray. In that order. Menus against the wall. Everything in its place.

"I sweep outside the front of the bar and get rid of any outdated posters on the bulletin board. At 8:30, I am at PNC bank to get the day's money. They have really good coffee there—different flavors—and it's free. I usually get the caramel vanilla.

"Finally, I make my phone calls, like to Fountain Products. I chat with Dianna and order to-go containers, cups, saran wrap and stuff. Then, there's beer and food deliveries—I am there for all that. When everything is settled, I sit down in my booth—fourth one from the back—and read the morning paper. Or, at least I used to. In October, 2019, they stopped with the daily paper—only three days a week now. That's really messing up my thing. I do my word finder and watch TV. I have soup, play pinball and sometimes there's a free song or two left on the jukebox.

"That's one of the perks of working here. The pinball and the jukebox. Like, there is this one guy that hates the song *Atomic Dog*. So, when he's there, I make sure I play it. It's my little way of getting back at him for being rotten. Then there's the fact that we have AC all summer long and heat in the winter. Plus, there are three TVs, the food is great and I literally meet someone new every day.

"Another thing I do is wipe the ledge outside under the window. People do their scratch-offs there that they buy next door at the newsstand. There's always a lot of that gummy stuff; it's hard to wipe off. And then for a while there, there was the bird lady who left breadcrumbs for the birds on the ledge. Not birds, pigeons. I told her to stop; the crumbs and the pigeon poop were disgusting. She kept right on doing it until I followed her up to the coffee shop and told her I was going to call the cops. Sometimes you have to do these things. I never saw her again.

"At exactly 11 a.m., I open the door. Steve is usually my first customer. He's my 'Norm,' my longest returning customer in 40 years. I think of Steve as family. I mean, I've watched his kids grow up. Usually Steve orders his iced tea, and either a BLT or a cup of chili & garlic bread. I swear, he's like a magnet; he attracts people and talks to all of them.

"He knows a lot. You can ask Steve almost anything and if he doesn't know, he'll find out and come back with your answer tomorrow. Don't get me wrong, he can be cranky. Like, he refused to write a page for this book because he said we were just saying nice things about The Cage—none of the dirt. There's dirt for ya, Steve.

"Usually Steve is joined by Jim. That's when I put the coffee on. Jim likes a fresh cup. Then some days Gus and Ed join them in the corner by the window under the TV. I call it my Old Man's Corner.

Over the years, I have also developed a few pet peeves. Like snot rags. I mean, can you even imagine someone blowing their nose and then leaving it on their plate? It's disgusting. I've told people to throw their own tissues away or take it with them. They look at me like I'm crazy, but I'm serious. I'm not touching that.

Old Man's Corner

"Then, there was this one time a bicycle guy came in; a bunch of his buddies were joining him for drinks. I got his beer and when I came back, a woman had joined him. He put out this moldy $10 bill to pay for the beers and I told him I was not touching that thing. He said it was in his back pocket so it was OK, but you could see the black on it. The woman ended up paying and all of his friends were calling him Mr. Moldy by the time they left. They were good tippers.

"The last thing is my pens. People steal 'em. I try to keep lots of them handy, but people don't think and they walk off with them. It makes me crazy.

"Then there are some cool things, like one time this woman came in with a 5-carat diamond. I had never seen anything like it. I'll never forget it. Sometimes people have foreign coins and I like to keep them. I never traveled out of the U.S., but I have coins from all over the world. Oh, and I remember the first time I saw a gay guy dressed to the hilt. He had short shorts and a fishnet tank top. When I turned to get a closer look, he had nipple rings. I know it doesn't sound like much anymore, but back then it sure did open my eyes.

"Then there was Ruthie. She was always drunk and I couldn't serve her. She wore this big fur coat everywhere. The line I remember the most was. 'You know how many men I had to fuck to get this coat?' That's just how Ruthie was. I haven't seen her for years. Hope she's OK.

"I think over the years it has gone something like this: In the beginning I felt like Dorothy in Oz—everything was so new and interesting and exciting. Then it became more like The Twilight Zone when I think of all the weird shit I've seen. But in the end, it's The Bermuda Triangle. It's a mystery what will happen next. People disappear (and reappear) all the time."

I guess it's always really been "As The Cage Turns." That kind of says it all.

OPEN BOTTLE
HERE

GENTLEMEN
CUSTOMER
PARKING ONLY
LADIES

THE SQUIRREL HILL
CAFE
PITTSBURGH, PA.
521-3327

Best Dressed Man in the Bar

Molly & David

Max

Ann & Tim

Jewish Community Center Regulars

Parking

"It's not the heat, it's the humidity." That's what every yinzer knows about August in Pittsburgh. It was a can of soup out there when I left the cool auditorium at Carnegie Mellon University, where my nephew had just played the hell out of a trumpet.

After an encore and a raucous improv, I hugged my nephew and his boyfriend goodbye and stepped out of the institutionalized AC into the thick of it, keeping my arms elevated slightly to avoid the impending stickiness as I hiked across the campus, passing the legendary CMU fence on my way to the car.

The fence is like a billboard layered with years of protests and celebrations, challenges and cheers. Painted in the dark of night and guarded by the artists until they are willing to forfeit their statement, it greets students in the morning with messages ranging from witty to poignant. Because of its highly visible location, it is an ideal place to proclaim/advertise almost anything. That day, the fence said, "Hot Stuff." Not inspired, not claimed, not even noteworthy, but true.

So, the AC in my car sucks and there is no escaping the dreaded "moist." I have a window unit at home, but that mostly means sitting in front of it naked to get relief. I'm thinking it might be nice to stop off somewhere until the sun does its daily dance down the sky and things cool off.

Driving up Forbes Avenue, I edge up to Squirrel Hill, with its lovely old mansion homes, big trees, synagogues and bustling business district. I grew up walking to Squirrel Hill from my rattier neighborhood home in Wilkinsburg about a mile away. When I was a teenager, my friends and I would trek the stretch of Forbes from Braddock Avenue in search of bagels and ice cream. I didn't know that bagels were a Jewish food then, just that they were wonderful and only a quarter at the Bagel Nosh. Then, there was Baskin-Robbins. Needless to say, we never walked off the calories we consumed, but we had a lot of fun doing it; Squirrel Hill was always a treat.

Mind you, I didn't have to park back then and it never occurred to me that parking would finally determine my treat accessibility or that alcohol would become my treat of choice. So, at Wightman, I start playing the parking game. Here's the deal: if there is a parking spot—a close parking spot—close meaning in the first-half block of Forbes after the Murray intersection (no U-turns, no side streets, certainly not the garage), but a parking spot with my name on it, only then will I stop at The Squirrel Hill Cafe (heretofore known as The Cage).

Sure, I had a lot of important shit to get done like binge-watching *Brooklyn Nine-Nine*, but I'm thinking it's hot, I'm jazzed and The Cage is cool. I'm thinking, "Please, let there be a parking space."

Sure enough, call it destiny, call it karma, call it whatever, I'm pulling up to the light at Forbes and Murray where The Cage sits right after the corner landmark, Cold Stone Creamery, and there it is, calling out to me with a grand, vacant gesture: a wide, empty stretch of pavement right in front of The Squirrel Hill Newsstand, next door to The Cage. Fate at its finest.

I put my turn signal on, pulled in (which I suck at, by the way; give me parallel parking any time), got out, paid the meter with my handy mobile app and strolled down the sidewalk to the glorious red door—the iconic, welcoming beacon sirening "The Squirrel Hill Cafe."

In all honesty, any excuse to go to The Cage is eventually justified: the sweet juxtaposition of decadent/defeatist and deserving. (Think Sheryl Crow's "All I Wanna Do," based on poet Wyn Cooper's "Fun"). You're bound to engage in or witness something memorable, or simply feel the weight of the workweek drain from your glass. Something about the down lighting, the big windows, the smoke, the fryer grease, the occasional burst of unchecked laughter. It's always good. And if you're the talky type, there's always someone to chat up.

It was Saturday, so I knew Jan would be there; she has worked every Saturday at The Cage since before time. Ends up nearly 40 years she has worked there—40 years! That's a long time to be slinging drinks. That's a lot of stories.

A Drink in the Dark

I met Jan in 1982 when I first started working at The Cage. In total, I spent 10 years behind the bar, and now, more than 20 in front of it. Something keeps me coming back when I'm feeling good—and bad. It isn't fancy, more a neighborhood tavern in an unexpected place—diamond in the rough. Like I said, Squirrel Hill is pretty upscale with boutique shops, nice restaurants and a fair amount of money. Lots of doctors, lawyers and academics, but you'd be surprised how the demographic stretches when you put a comfortable, welcoming watering hole in the center of it.

So, when I pushed open the red door that thick August afternoon, it was with a certain joy and relaxed anticipation—an hour to myself with a nice drink, a cigarette and the cool, dark calm of The Cage. It wasn't crowded, but it also wasn't empty—kind of typical for a Saturday afternoon at 4 p.m. In fact, I don't know I have ever seen The Cage empty except late at night, after close, with the barstools upside down on the bar like a crown, neon lighting the end of another shift. It's a nice kind of empty, like walking through Kennywood Park after it closes, the remnants of the day's excitement in the air, the ghost of laughter and ruckus, the echo of glasses clinking in a toast to a new start. It's the juxtaposition of quiet in a space usually brimming with clamor that makes the bar after close so special. Makes you feel special. A drink in the dark.

As I walked into the cozy, dim din, Jan immediately waved from behind the bar and raised her finger to indicate, "just give me a moment." She misses nothing. Small and tough, Jan doesn't take shit and is as honest as you can be in a world that makes it easier to lie. She's quick to smile and has a laugh that is from the heart. Not the belly, the heart. She's also 68, and as noted, spent nearly 40 of her years at The Cage. Jan is almost religious about the attention she pays to her customers—no one goes unnoticed for more than two minutes and she's always up for a story, which most are more than ready to share. She smokes a lot, but doesn't drink (a rarity in the bar industry) and has a touch of necessary OCD. Her bar is never messy. She knows where everything is.

For all the years that I worked at the bar and those that came after, Jan has been a friend, a confidante, a comfort and enigma. Mothers should not be friends and friends should not be mothers, but Jan has always been both to me. She is wise in ways that are unflinching. She is pragmatic and brusque, but open and listening; vulnerable in a beautiful, hard-ass way. She is also intrinsically funny.

So, while Jan's finishing up a sale, I find a seat at the bar where I can keep an eye on the door, but also see out the windows—you never know what you could miss. The TV is on mute, probably airing some sporting activity (it almost always is) but nobody cares unless it's the Steelers, the Penguins or, possibly, the Pirates.

Settling in, it wouldn't be a stretch to say I felt at home, because I was. Not just because I have worked here, but because it is, perhaps, the most comfortable, diverse, nonjudgmental bar in Pittsburgh. Think Planet Fitness with cocktails.

You can start a conversation with anyone from a landscaper to a lawyer, or just read a book, and never worry about anything. I think the key word here is *safe.* You are always safe at The Cage. Plus, the nostalgic smell of smoke and fryer grease gets me every time—the jukebox playing everything from Beyoncé to Meatloaf.

I nod to a couple of regulars, who I know from my days behind the bar, and I pick up my phone and pretend I am doing something millennial-like. Jan gives the bar another once-over to make sure everyone is good, hands me my legacy greyhound in a tall glass and then sits beside me. She lights up—literally and figuratively.

. . .

> "I have been wanting to talk to you," she says. "And here you are. I want to write a book about The Cage …"

Pause.

> "You should do that; such rich material. You must have so many stories, characters," I said. And then she said, "I want you to write it with me."

I didn't flinch or take a sip or a drag. I didn't think about my full plate—work, freelance, volunteering, momming—or expectations. I didn't think about everything I would have to ask for, commit to, that I would have to invest in. I didn't think about this chapter or how to make you want to read it. I just heard myself say "yes."

I knew there was already a book out about The Cage, written by a former bartender. I also knew it was pretty nasty, but just from hearsay. Jan told me there was a copy for a buck in the used book bin across the street at the library, but that I shouldn't waste my money. She gave me the bar copy to take home.

Indeed, the book, *Cage Days: A Fluid Novel,* was, in fact, pretty awful. Fluid in the sense that it was mean, like lava or boiling oil or something. It was certainly not nice. It denigrated everyone in the bar, except perhaps, the author himself and his wife, who also worked there. Shameless and gross in some ways, it was self-aggrandizing, complete with typos.

A lot of Jan's motivation to write another Cage book was to make this wrong right, to tell the story of The Cage from the people's perspective, the customers and the employees who worked there—to set Ronnie's reputation straight (Ronnie DeLallo was the owner of The Cage for 30+ years). So yeah, no. You will find no masturbatory scenes of fucking a woman in the basement only to leave here there because she wore a prosthetic ...

That said, I am not a journalist or a prose writer; I am certainly not a researcher. I am a poet, but I know a good story when I see one. Jan's nearly 40 years at The Cage are rife with local culture—stories of people I love and don't—the people of Pittsburgh, the residents of Squirrel Hill, the regulars, the transients, the university professors, the drunks, the lonley(s), the students, the workers and the passers-by that make The Squirrel Hill Cafe what it is and always has been—the quintessential melting pot of Pittsburgh—a community within a community.

I've always thought that if you've never been to The Cage, you've never really been to Pittsburgh, and now I was being given the opportunity to share that truism. How could I say "no"? I still dream about working there. The beauty of pure physical labor for eight hours, the dumbwaiter, Ronnie telling me I had to be more of a hard-ass, late nights with Billy after the bar closed. So much of my own history is wrapped up in this place. I have worked here. I have cried here. I have written poems here. I have met every lover here. I have recommended it

to every person who comes to town who doesn't mind smoke... And, honestly, I almost always find a parking spot.

John at the jukebox

Debbie

Little's Shoes lunch

Josh Hecke

Ron & Slim

Road Trip: Hard Road

On Sunday, August 20, 2017, Jan picked me up at 10 a.m. (I talked her down from 7 a.m.) and we headed off to her cabin in Everett, PA, between Bedford & Breezewood. I had never really had "alone time" with Jan short of conversations at the bar, but it never occurred to me that things would go any different than they did. From the second I got in the car, we never stopped—talking and driving and laughing.

We speak the same language, hers with a bit more Pittsburgh yinzer than mine, but still the same vernacular of blunt and beautiful truths. We talked about her hard life growing up in Swissvale. We talked about my hard life growing up in Wilkinsburg. Our hard fathers. Our hard choices. Our hard hearts. Our soft spots for men, our anger at our soft spots. Neither one of us ever had any money; we both have always been horribly self-reliant, working since the age of 12 or so. We bonded over our work ethic and a certain OCD about cleanliness and ashes.

I had my mom; Jan had her dad. Jan's mom had MS and her father worked three shifts at the steel mills to take care of her. Poor in money but not in spirit, we both had single parents who had to work a lot just to keep food on the table. We were latchkey kids with maybe too much freedom. We both hated school.

Jan got pregnant at 17 and gave birth to her son Larry six months before the night she should have graduated from high school. She married, got her GED and had Amy two years later.

My stepfather died when I was 13 and my mother sort of checked out for a few years. I didn't get into trouble—not more than smoking and sleeping with drop-outs—but I hated school and threatened to quit. Instead I got into early admissions at Carnegie Mellon University and started college at 17.

Having only one participatory parent, we learned to rely on ourselves; we knew nothing was going to fall out of the sky, working for everything we had. I think we learned this from our parents, who weren't there because they had to take care of us—financially if not emotionally.

An hour and a half in, we arrived at Jan's cabin (the safe, family getaway place) and I was introduced to a whole new side of Jan. So quiet, so rustic, so filled with quirky knick-knacks and the occasional cushion. It is her refuge, her secret, her escape. I felt honored that she shared it with me, that she was allowing me to share it with her. For a moment, I honestly wished I had one of my own, except I would need the Internet and maybe takeout.

After attending to a few summer-end tasks at the cabin, we headed to Jean Bonnet's on route 30, Jan's favorite respite, next to her cabin mecca. On the way, we stopped at her friend Carl's, who just happened to be outside and waved us into his home of many, many taxidermy specimens and jars of homemade jam that he generously shared—boysenberry.

It was a little later than we expected when we finally arrived at Jean Bonnet's. My only experience with this historic hotel was a number of years back when I had reservations to spend the night, but got scared off by the ghost stories that populate the residence. I remember the portabella salad was really good, and the beer. And then I remember needing to leave. They don't make a big deal about the spirits that have their home there, but it was eerie enough for me.

This, however, was the middle of a sunny, hot August afternoon and we sat outside on the patio. No ghosts except the stories we would come to tell that continue to haunt this book, in a good way, I think.

Our waitress was lovely. Her name was Mikayla. Jan asked if she could get the manager to come talk to us. Jan wanted him to know that THIS was the place that we were commemorating the start of The Cage book (which I had already decided was going to be called *The Red Door*). A devoted Jean Bonnet patron, Jan hands out brochures for the B&B to Cage patrons who are transient; she stocks up on them so she doesn't run out.

The Manager at Jean Bonnet was welcoming and excited about our writing adventure, and Mikayla came out to take our picture in front of the Jean Bonnet sign. She was going into the Marines, but asked if she could buy a copy of the book. We already had a sale. It was a done deal.

From then on, Jan and I met nearly every Monday to talk and record stories/memories/myths about the Cage. It was more about us. We would smoke, I would drink, and we became the kind of friends that don't hold anything back. I told her about my child transitioning. She understood. She told me about her daughter and grandchildren. I understood. We talked about love—a lot.

Jan has been with Bill for 30 years. She met him at The Cage back in the 1970s. He stopped in after he finished his classes at Rosedale Tech; they just started talking and that was that. He became her second husband. I, on the other hand, have never been married, though I had had a few great loves. We laughed about my dating exploits and imagined Jan moving in downstairs when we got older.

And, of course, we talked about Ronnie and the bar endlessly—something we both understood. We gave each other Christmas presents: a sweater to keep me warm (I am so cold), the picture of us at Jean Bonnet framed for Jan, and because Jan is Jan, chocolate chip cookies for my son and a beautiful ornament Jan's daughter Amy made with thousands of sequins. If nothing comes of this book, our love will pay the cost.

That was the beginning and we were in it 100%. I found the writing hard, but the goal, tangible. How would I express the ways the Squirrel Hill Cafe/The Cage has touched so many lives? Why does it matter? Because it does. It is part of our cultural landscape—retail, social and even political. Home away from home?

You decide.

On a hot summer's day quite a few years ago, I was walking along in Squirrel Hill. I ran into Jack, a former classmate of mine both at Linden and Allderdice High School. We hadn't seen each other in many years so we decided to stop in the Cafe for a few beers and many reminiscences. It occurred to us at the same time. "Why not phone the rest of our group and have a mini-reunion right here at the Squirrel Hill Cafe? There were only six of us so it shouldn't be that hard." As it turned out, it was a little difficult to locate everybody. We had all gone to college but different ones. Google was not yet available to help us.

Hooray! Everyone agreed to come. And they did! We sat down in the Squirrel Hill Cafe with beer flowing and mouths working to catch up on all those missing years. At closing time, we finally caught our breath as we were escorted out the door. We decided that this had been a great experience and we should do it again next year. But life doesn't often work that way. The writer, Thomas Wolfe, once wrote "You can't go home again." For the most part, he was right. We parted that night, each going in our own different direction. But the memory of our night at the Cafe stays in my mind and I suspect my friends feel the same way. The memories remain.

—Ernest M. Halle

Larry & Max

Jonathan

Alex

Billy & Ben

Liana

Jim

History All. The. Time.

Can you believe it? Digital copy of the original blueprint of the proposed facade designed for the Squirrel Hill Cafe, circa 1934. The blueprint was passed down from Elizabeth Paterni's estate upon her death, and now belongs to Michael Nieri. Elizabeth was the wife of Mike Paterni, owner of The Squirrel Hill Cafe from approximately 1918 to 1963, who passed away in 1957.

Mal Gianni, a younger brother of Elizabeth, graduated from Carnegie Tech School of Architecture and worked on these drawings while starting his practice in the City of Pittsburgh in the early 1930s. Take note that this drawing was given the title *The Italian Cafe for Mr. M. Paterni.*

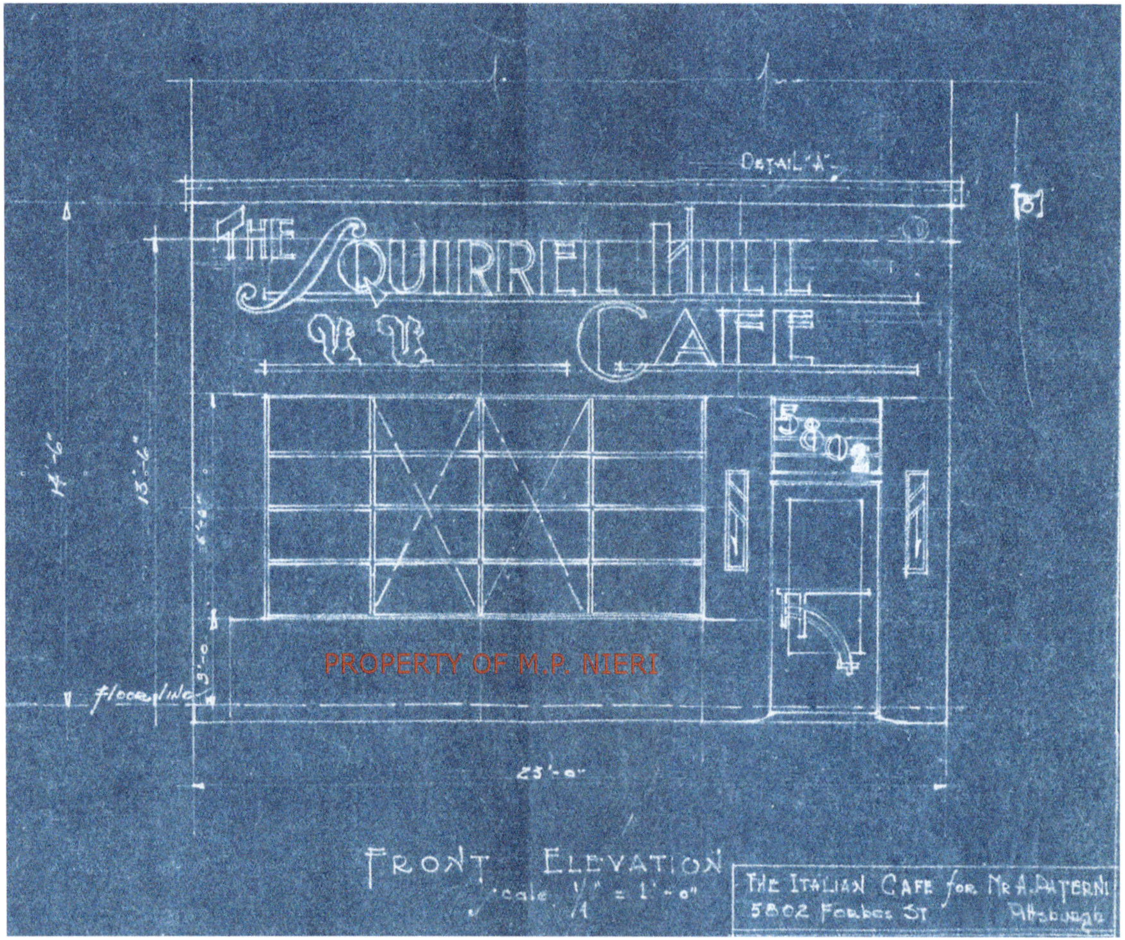

Truth be told, for 2½ years we worked stupid hard trying to uncover the history of The Cage. We knew what Jimmy DeLallo, Ronnie's brother, could tell us, and rumor had it that The Cage might have been a deli long ago ....

Hi Jan,

Thank you for your efforts to write this book and pay tribute to Ronnie's long and colorful tenure as manager of the Squirrel Hill Cafe.

A little history: The original owner of the SHC could probably be traced to the early 1900's.

In 1976, our dad, John DeLallo decided to purchase the SHC when owner George Sodini decided to retire from the business. After many years of keeping the books for Mr. Sodini, dad knew it was and would continue to be a thriving business.

Dad basically told my brother Dave and me that we were in the bar business. For the next four or five years, Dave and I worked opposite daylight and night shifts getting together Sundays for a serious clean-up of the bar. In 1981, when I decided to go to college, Dave and I brought Ronnie into the business and showed him the ropes.

Dave stayed another three or four years.

Looking back, it seems like Ronnie was there forever.

I guess he's still there in many ways.

For me, the SHC was always an adventure with many fond and a few not-so-fond memories. I met lots of interesting people there, including my first wife Mary.

It was all quite an education.

Sincerely,
Jimmy DeLallo

We went down to the Allegheny County deeds office to try and discover the history of the property. But the actual address, 5802 Forbes Avenue, appeared to be part of a larger parcel of land that includes Uncle Sam's Gourmet Subs, the newsstand and The Cage.

We Googled, we called the Squirrel Hill Historical Society, we asked everyone we knew. It was a sad wash and an embarrassing hole—until the final hour. Then, out of nowhere (or, in perfect Cage karma), a voicemail from Geraldine "Mac" McGartland.

Who's Mac?

"I was married to Walt Nieri, whose mother & Betty Paterni were sisters. Gianni is their birth/family name. Michael McGartland, my brother, occasionally visits the Squirrel Hill Cafe. He told Jan of my connection with the bar and asked me to call her. My married name was Geraldine Nieri, and after divorce returned to my birth name, Geraldine 'Mac' McGartland."

So, within 24 hours, we got an email from Walt Nieri, who, at 77, was totally networking with cc's and phone numbers.

Leslie,

Sorry for the delay!
You will get plenty of information from all 3 of these individuals!! The Cafe was under the ownership of my uncle and aunt (Mike and Elizabeth Paterni) for many years. Jack (my brother) and John (my nephew) have a lot of information regarding it (including menus, articles etc.); both are the historians of our family! Jerry (my cousin) worked there for several years and can obviously provide great additional information.

We are always happy that someone is writing about the Squirrel Hill Cafe (a place that was close to our family for many of years).

Love to see the final version!!
Walt

Wanting desperately to write THE definitive book about The Cage, this was a godsend, a coup, a true Cage moment. Because these things happen there. All. The. Time. My "for instance": You walk in. You sit down. You see a woman looking thoughtful, alone, quiet. And, the next thing you know you are talking to Megan, wife of Pittsburgh's rockin' Karl Hendricks, who owned Sound Cat records in Bloomfield and was known all over for his uber-indie Karl Hendricks Trio. He died of oral cancer in 2017 and it was a sad day for Pittsburgh. Megan is still going through all of his stuff. And, of course, it's the same Megan who was your best friend's friend. But they had a falling out … You exchange phone numbers.

It happens all of the time.

So, as Cage fate would have it, Michael (Mac's brother) stops at The Cage, talks to Jan, talks to his sister, who calls Jan, who calls me and gives my number to Mac; then, Mac sends her ex (Walt Nieri) an email and he emails his brother Jack and nephew John, and in 2 weeks, we fill in 45 years of missing Cage history. Thank goodness we had the lumbering publishing pace to wait it out!

The whole family: so generous with their research and knowledge, clippings and photos and …

… THIS BEAUTIFUL TIMELINE!

Squirrel Hill Fruit Store Vannucci & Partner	1916
Death: Vannucci & Partner	1918
Paterni & Rossini	1918
Prohibition / Paterni	1920-1933
Squirrel Hill Cafe / Paterni	1934
George Sodini	1963
John DeLallo	1976
Patty & Rod Oliverio	2007

My first email from Jack Nieri was super informative—and exciting!

My brother Walt Nieri contacted me by email informing me that you are doing research on the SHC. My aunt and uncle (Michael and Elizabeth Paterni) owned the business around 45 years between the 1920s and 1980s. I have photos, family info and memories of that store. Most of my familiarity with the operation was between the years of 1950 and 1970. My aunt and mother were sisters in the Pittsburgh "Gianni" family.

What I remember about the cafe was the dumbwaiter behind the bar where they could lower the empty bottles to the basement. My uncle also used it to drop loose coins to the lower floor in bags. The basement looked like the Philadelphia mint. I used to get a week's vacation at their home at 2529 Beechwood Blvd. when I was 6 to 10 years of age. My uncle would let me wrap/roll all of the pennies, which I enjoyed doing. I was allowed to keep the Indian heads.

In summer, 1957, after my uncle died, I worked for two weeks as a bartender for my aunt. Dominick, the regular bartender, wanted time off for his vacation. I knew very little about tending bar but had to learn quickly to satisfy the customers.

When I arrived at 7:30 a.m. there was a line-up at the door waiting for me. They expected me to know what they drank; it took me two days to catch on. With a dozen or so guys at the bar drinking, I had to learn to keep track of how many drinks and the amount to charge them. Very challenging, to say the least. If I recall, I managed to perfect my work after the fourth day.

There were four tiers at the back bar: the bottom contained the 25¢ shots, 35¢ shots were on the next shelf, 45¢ and 55¢+ on the top shelf. Rock & Rye was a big seller then. Corby's was on the bottom shelf. Most of the men were on their way to work in the morning and at 4:00 p.m. most of them returned to wet their whistle. My aunt said that when prohibition began, uncle Mike brought in musicians and nightly entertainment for the college crowd. The store was remodeled and the mezzanine used for space.

Serving hot dogs became an "in" thing and brought a lot of customers. In 1934, when prohibition ended, the business was changed to a cafe serving 3 meals a day and alcohol.

During the Christmas holidays, 1961, I returned to work at the Cafe to help my aunt. Things had changed a bit and the old hard-liquor folks were no longer around. Still, if these walls could talk, there would be a great story written about "Life @ the Cafe." (Foreshadowing.)

My aunt and uncle were like second parents to me and our families spent many Sundays together. My uncle was a very kind and generous man and my aunt was a good cook. It's a combination that's hard to beat!!

*—**Jack***

Printed on Feb 9, 2020

Squirrel Hill Fruit Co., 5802 Forbes st., rt.
Squirrel Hill Fruit Co., 5802 Forbes st., eh.

Squirrel Hill Fruit Co.

DINNERS

T-Bone Steak, Potatoes, Vegetables	.60
Steak, Potatoes, Vegetables, Mushrooms or Onions	.75
Pork Chops, Vegetables, Potatoes	.50
Breaded Veal Cutlet, Vegetables, Potatoes	.40
Baked Ham, Potatoes, Vegetables	.35
Roast Pork or Beef, Potatoes, Vegetables	.35
Ham or Bacon and Eggs, Potatoes, Vegetables	.35
Hamburger Steak, Potatoes, Vegetables	.25
SPECIAL — SPAGHETTI, Meat Sauce	.35
SPAGHETTI, Mushroom Sauce	.40
RAVIOLI	.35

Soup .... .10 Pie .... .10

OMELETS

HAM, CHEESE, ONION, or SPANISH
Includes Potatoes, Vegetables .... .35

SANDWICHES

Baked Ham (our special)	.10	Pimento Cheese	.10
Squirrel Hill Special	.20	Fried Ham, Lettuce, Tomato	.15
Italian Salami	.10	Bacon, Lettuce, Tomato	.15
Mortadella	.10	Western	.15
Combination	.20	Club	.30
Fried Egg	.10	Steak	.35
Sardine	.15	Lettuce and Tomato	.10
Hamburger	.10	Tuna Fish	.15
Hot Dog	.10	Cold Roast Pork	.15
Swiss Cheese	.10	Cold Roast Beef	.15

Hot Roast Pork or Beef, Potatoes, Gravy .... .20

SALADS

Combination — Italian Style, Shrimp, Tuna Fish, Crab Meat,
Salmon, Chicken, or Lettuce and Tomato .... .35
Potato .... 10 .... Cole Slaw .... .10

COCKTAILS

Dry Martini	.25	Side Car	.35
Manhattan	.25	Bacardi	.35
Orange Blossom	.25	Alexander	.35
Bronx	.25	Clover Club	.35
Old Fashioned	.30	Dubonnet	.30
Pink Lady	.30	Paterni's Hot Punch	.25

MIXED DRINKS

Gin Buck	.20	Gin Sour	.25
Gin Rickey	.20	Whiskey Sour	.30
Gin Fizz	.25	Brandy Sour	.35
Sloe Gin Rickey or Fizz	.25	Silver or Golden Fizz	.30
Tom Collins	.25	Royal Fizz	.35
High Ball	25 - 30 - 35	Egg nogg Brandy or Whiskey	.35

WHISKEYS

Green River	.10	Guckenheimer	.10	Four "X"	.15
Kessler's	.10	Bottoms Up	.10	Wilson's	.15
Sherbrook	.10	Tom Walker	.10	Seagram's "5"	.15
Town Tavern	.10	Penn State	.10	Irish American	.15
Cream of Kent	.10	Paul Jones	.15	Penn Maryland	.15
Hiram Green	.10	Calvert's Reserve	.15	Three Feathers	.15
Crab Orchard	.10	Old Oscar Pepper	.15	Seagram's "7"	.20
Old Drum	.10	Old Farm	.15	Black Lable	.20
Cobb's Creek	.10	Golden Wedding	.15	Four Roses	.20
Old Man	.10	Gibson's	.15	Sam Thompson	.20
Frantz Special	.10	Thos. Moore	.15	Dillinger	.20
Old Quaker	.10	Mattingly & Moore	.15	Chicken Cock	.20

BONDED WHISKEYS		SPIRITS	
Seagram's "83"	.25	Sloe Gin	.15
Seagram's Ancient Bottle	.25	Apple Jack	.20
Mount Vernon	.25	Carioca Rum	.20
Old Overholt	.25	Bacardi Rum	.35
Green River	.25	Jamaca Rum	.30
Gibson's	.25	Martel — 3 star	.30
Canadian Club	.25	Hennessy — 3 star	.35

CORDIALS

Kimmel	.15	Vermouth	.20
Rock and Rye	.15	Benedictine	.20
Anisette	.20	Cherry	.20
Apricot	.20	Peach	.20
Creme-De-Cacro	.20	Creme-De-Menthe	.20

Contreau .... .20

Excerpts from original Squirrel Hill Cafe menu, circa 1935

Pittsburgh Post-Gazette

Pittsburgh Post-Gazette (Pittsburgh, Pennsylvania) · 28 Apr 1934, Sat · Page 29

Downloaded on Feb 9, 2020

SPAGHETTI DINNERS—Beers, whisky, ale. Paterni Restaurant, 5802 Forbes st. Jackson 9904.

The first time I talked with Jack, it was for an hour on a Monday night. He is Italian. I'm half. He's dropping names all from Lucca, Italy: Poli, Tambellini, Sodini, Gianni, Nardi, all Italian immigrants who made Pittsburgh their home. He's talking

Jack, age 12, with Uncle Mike Paterni, circa 1950

about how Uncle Mike and Poli were buddies, how Nardi taught some of the best chefs in Pittsburgh, how Mal Gianni designed the blueprints for the front of the cafe. He talked about how close-knit their family was—and still is.

At some point, we accidentally FaceTimed and it was so lovely to see such generosity of spirit and energy and excitement about sharing the family legacy.

The upshot is that The Cage began as a fruit stand established by Alfred (Frank) Vannucci in 1916 (see p. 36 for citizenship application).

Then this from John (Jack's nephew).

Uncle Jack,
It looks like the Squirrel Hill Fruit Market at 5802 Forbes was started by Frank Vannucci in about 1916. It had to be part of the "Lucca fruit & Confectionery" crew that we know and love. Mike Paterni appeared to be working there by 1918. Frank and his business partner BOTH died on October 5, 1918 from influenza. Not making this up. Both young.

Frank Vannucci was from Lucca I believe (but not certain). Mike Paterni was the executor of Frank's will and reopened the store in 1919. He had a partner, Paul Rossini, until about 1921. Paul was the new husband of Frank Vannucci's widow, Argentina Vannucci. I guess for two years it operated under the

PARTNERS DIE OF PNEUMONIA

Long Business Association Will Culminate in Double Funeral.

INFLUENZA VICTIMS

A double funeral for two Italians, partners in business for more than 10 years, and who died within eight hours, victims of pneumonia which developed from Spanish influenza, will be held this afternoon. Interment will be made in Calvary Cemetery.

The victims of the dreaded disease are Dominic Taterni, aged 28, and Frank Vannucci, aged 31, of 6410 Phillips avenue. They were stricken with influenza last Tuesday and were removed to St. John's Hospital. Taterni died Friday night and his partner died early Saturday morning.

The two men came to the United States 14 years ago. Three years later they established a fruit store in Smithfield street where the new Chamber of Commerce Building now stands. They later moved their store to Forbes street and Murray avenue, where they conducted the business until last Tuesday, when the store was closed after the partners had been removed to the hospital.

Vannucci leaves a widow and two children. Taterni was unmarried.

John McIntosh seated on original Squirrel Hill Cafe chair, circa 1940

business name of "Rossini & Paterni." Paul Rossini was apparently a WWI war hero.

And yes, Jerry is on-point with respect to the name changing to The Squirrel Hill Cafe in 1935 after prohibition was repealed in Dec. 1934. 1935 was also the year Mike built the house on 2529 Beechwood Blvd. The design of the house was gifted to Liz by her brother Mal Gianni, a graduate of Carnegie Tech.

Fast forward 100+ years after its founding by Lucca immigrants, and Anthony Bourdain films his "Parts Unknown" Pittsburgh episode in the SHC in June 2017.
100 years of stories.
-John (McIntosh)

And then Jerry, who actually worked at The Squirrel Hill Cafe (or the SHC as the cool, inside family people call it):

Leslie, my name is Jerry Gianni. I am Walter's cousin. I worked at the Squirrel Hill Cafe starting in 1957; I was 17 years old. My uncle Mike had died and Elizabeth called my father to see if my brother could work at the bar to cover the vacations of her bartenders. My brother was 21 years old, but he was in the service. My dad sent me instead.

I wasn't old enough to drink, but it was fairly easy since a mixed drink in The Cage was a shot and a beer back then. My Aunt sold the cafe in either in 1962 or 1963. I graduated college and left for California in 1963.

There were two brothers who were bartenders: Dominick the day bartender who said he had worked there for 35 years, which means he started there in 1925 or 1927; and Patsy was there 25 years. The Cage was in business pre-Prohibition that ran from 1920 to 1933. I would assume that The Cage became a bar shortly after prohibition. Some even said that it was a speak-easy.

We served three menus a day, breakfast, lunch and dinner. We served a sausage sandwich and a beer for 55¢. A shot in those days was 25¢. We had a 12 oz. coke for a dime. Hopefully this is helpful.

—Jerry Gianni

One thing we realized after all was said and done was that none of us knew anything about George Sodini, whom Liz Paterni sold the café to in 1963. But that only made Jack & John more determined.

Said Jack:
My aunt Betty said that George was a good cook and was, prior to SHC, a chef at Tambellini's on Wilkins Ave. We are still on the hunt to find out how she found him to take over the business. Every family that came from Lucca has at least one Tambellini mixed in their family. In Lucca, they are like the Smiths here.

There was actually NOT a Tambellini's restaurant on Wilkins Avenue, but there WAS Sodini's Bar & Grill (1932-1990 or so, originally co-owned by brothers Orlando Joseph, Charles and Paul Sodini) on the corner of Wilkins Ave. and Wightman, where a CVS now stands. George, a cousin of the Sodinis, was hired as head chef. The bar and grill became Sodini's Restaurant in the early 1960s and George bought The Squirrel Hill Cafe in 1963. He did, in fact, marry a Tambellini: Josephine Marie Tambellini. Rumor has it that although an Italian restaurant, Sodini's made the best Devonshire in the city. Perhaps, thanks to George.

Another cool and quirky thing about finding the Nieris was John McIntosh's collection of newspaper clippings pertaining to the café: "Thieves Work on Safe; Get Nothing," "Maid Takes Poison after Losing Job," "Young Mother Pays $50 Numbers Fine," and the best, "Two Liquor Licenses Revoked Here."

Anyone who has ever worked in the restaurant/hospitality industry knows that the door is always open and so are the possibilities for just about anything to happen. Incidences that paint the past with a wee bit of color just give The Cage even more character. And, seeing the photos, you can't help but feel that swank and grit still permeate the walls with a tarnished swagger. From baked ham and gin rickeys to cheeseburgers and Dogfish, The Cage has continued to deliver.
All. The. Time.

st-Gazette The Pittsburgh Press (Pittsburgh, Pennsylvania) · 11 Oct 1934, Thu · Page 26
Printed on Feb 9, 2020

MAID TAKES POISON AFTER LOSING JOB

Domestic Despondent — Fired Because She's Too Weak to Work

Fired from her job as a domestic because she was too weak to work, an 18-year-old Duquesne girl drank poison in a Squirrel Hill restaurant today rather than face the family she had been supporting on her $7-a-week salary.

Lillian Holstrom, of 1118 Barbour Street, Duquesne, was dismissed this morning by a Forbes Street housewife who told her she was too "delicate" to do the cleaning properly.

Despondent, she walked into the restaurant of Mike Paternis, 5802 Forbes Street and drained the contents of a small bottle.

She was taken to Homeopathic Hospital. Her condition is fair.

Pittsburgh Post-Gazette The Pittsburgh Press (Pittsburgh, Pennsylvania) · 5 Oct 1934, Fri · Page 51
Printed on Feb 9, 2020

YOUNG MOTHER PAYS $50 NUMBERS FINE

Woman With Two Children Arrested in Cafe

A young East End woman, the mother of two children, was fined $50 in East End Police Court today for writing numbers after she had testified two plainsclothesmen had taken $21 from her and only turned over $7.39 as evidence.

The plainsclothesmen, Louis Elford and James McGuire, said the $7.39 was all she had in her purse when arrested.

The officers told Magistrate Charles A. Papale they were sitting in a booth in a restaurant at 5802 Forbes Street when the woman, Mrs. Anna Stewart, 25, of 5915 Harvard Street, came to the next booth and started "writing" numbers.

Mrs. Stewart told Magistrate Papale she was only "a pickup girl" who turned her numbers over to "Roberts," who in turn gave them to "Robert Lindsey." Most of her numbers, she said, were received in the Wilkinsburg restaurant where she is employed.

Busted for Writing Numbers at 5802 Forbes, young East End woman, 1934

Clipped By:
mcintosh_john
Sun, Feb 9, 2020

Copyright © 2020 Newspapers.com. All Rights Reserved. Newspapers

Pittsburgh Post-Gazette The Pittsburgh Press (Pittsburgh, Pennsylvania) · 26 Mar 1943, Fri · Page 45
Printed on Feb 10, 2020

good wage. Sterling 3064.
WAITRESS—Over 21. Call at Squirrel Hill Cafe, 5802 Forbes St.
WAITRESS—Apply 728 Warrington Ave.

Pittsburgh Post-Gazette Pittsburgh Sun-Telegraph (Pittsburgh, Pennsylvania) · 8 Apr 1941, Tue · Page 14
Printed on Feb 9, 2020

2 Liquor Licenses Revoked Here

Two Pittsburgh district liquor licenses were revoked and 10 suspended by the State Liquor Control Board in Harrisburg. They are effective April 11.

Revocations were: Bernard Spitzer, 1101 Boston Avenue, distributor's license; Tioga & Braddock Restaurant, 7610 Tioga Street.

The suspensions: Frank George, Frank George's Inn, 106 Hillside Avenue, Turtle Creek, 20 days; Mrs. Anna Vrebac, Belgrade Bar & Grill, 201-205 Sandusky Street, 30 days; Frank and Regina Cremona, New Deal Restaurant, 208 Braddock Avenue, Turtle Creek, 10 days.

Uhro-Russian Club, Wilpen, 30 days; S. Herman Wolfe, Wolfe's Place, East Poland Avenue, Bessemer, 20 days; Mrs. Rina Meucci and John Meucci, 2907 Brownsville Road, Brentwood, 10 days; Louis Carletti, L. Carletti's, 403 East Third Avenue, Homestead, 10 days, distributor's license.

Michael Paterni, Squirrel Hill Cafe, 5802 Forbes Street, 10 days; Henry Schiavo, Broadway Restaurant, Coraopolis, 20 days; Tony Malanos, Tony Malanos' Lunch, 4 Milford Street, Duquesne, 20 days.

Licensees may pay fines in lieu of suspension.

Liquor license suspended for 10 days, Squirrel Hill Cafe

Washington rd., Mt. Lebanon. 913e
GIRLS (two) to work in confectionery and light lunchroom. 5802 Forbes st., Squirrel Hill. 913b
WHITE girl for general housework small

Help needed. 5802 Forbes, 1927

Rd., Squirrel Hill Highland Park

"IF YOU DON'T LIKE SPAGHETTI TRY OUR SPAGHETTI"

Says George Sodini, new owner of the Squirrel Hill Cafe. Other specialties — Ravioli, Veal Scaloppini alla Marsala, Shrimp, Steak. Not fancy but good.

REASONABLE PRICES

5802 Forbes Ave. Phone 521-9912

Mike & Liz Paterni at home.

Thieves Work On Safe; Get Nothing

Thieves who cracked their way into a Squirrel Hill tavern, then spent several hours knocking the combination from a safe Sunday night, had nothing to show for all th-- trouble, Squirrel Hill police reported.

The break-in and attempted robbery was reported by Mike Paternia, owner of the Squirrel Hill Cafe at 5902 Forbes Street, near the corner of Murray Avenue.

The thieves gained entrance to the cafe by breaking into a ladies washroom, then entering the main part of the bar and restaurant. Police said Paternia told them he had not used the safe for many years and had been unable to get it open for some time.

Mike Paterni's niece & nephews: Jack Nieri, Joan McIntosh & Walt Nieri

The safe referenced in the article is still in the basement today

* * *

MIKE PATERNI -- manager of the Squirrel Hill Cafe -- is just about ready to move into that new red tiled roofed home of his on Beechwood Boulevard. They say it is a beaut. We'll have to drop around and give it the once over. It is built of stone and there is a whisper that Mike will have a butler at the door.

* * *

Then & Now

Same angle.
5802 Forbes Ave. 2020.

5802 Forbes Ave., circa 1918 (look close and you can see the sign that says "Lunch Confectionary," assumedly Vannucci's place. From the book *Squirrel Hill* prepared by the Squirrel Hill Historical Society and published by Arcadia Publishing.

Back of bar, circa 1940. Man being served is owner, Mike Paterni. The server is Raymond Gianni, who was ordained as a Roman Catholic Priest in 1944. He is the brother of Liz Paterni and worked at the café while he was in seminary. In the background (L to R) is Dominick the bartender, Patsy the cook and a mystery server.

Back of bar 2020

History Clips

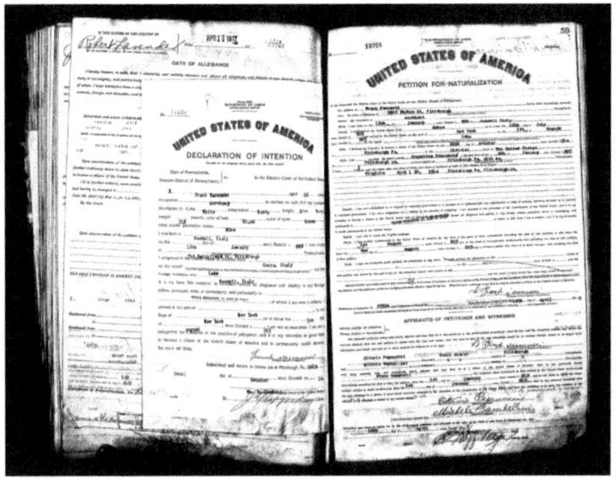

Immigration Papers, Frank Vennucci

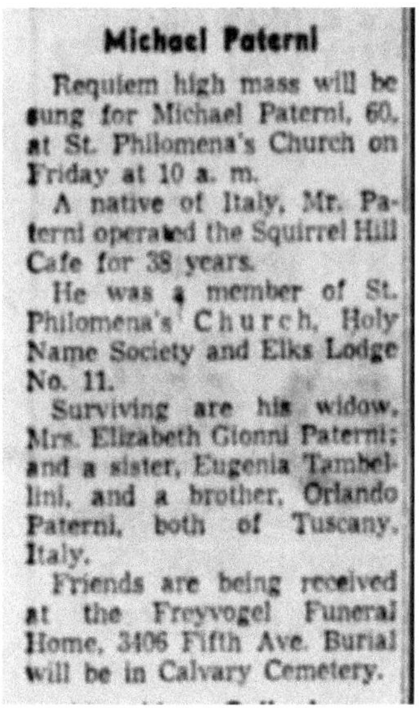

Michael Paterni

Requiem high mass will be sung for Michael Paterni, 60, at St. Philomena's Church on Friday at 10 a. m.

A native of Italy, Mr. Paterni operated the Squirrel Hill Cafe for 38 years.

He was a member of St. Philomena's Church, Holy Name Society and Elks Lodge No. 11.

Surviving are his widow, Mrs. Elizabeth Gionni Paterni; and a sister, Eugenia Tambellini, and a brother, Orlando Paterni, both of Tuscany, Italy.

Friends are being received at the Freyvogel Funeral Home, 3406 Fifth Ave. Burial will be in Calvary Cemetery.

Obituary, Michael Paterni

PITTSBURG HERO REACHES NEW YORK

By United Press.

New York, Dec. 23.—Among the heroes of the war returning on transports were two Pennsylvanians in the ranks who won honors at Verdun, Soissons and St. Michiel.

Private Paul Rossini of Co. H. Three Hundred and Twenty-eighth infantry, from Pittsburg, stood in the background modestly shielding his French decoration when a United Press man boarded the transport. No coaxing could make him tell the reason for the decoration. Finally some brothers in arms volunteered.

Rossini, according to their stories, was merely one of them up to 3:30 o'clock on Sept. 23. At that hour he sneaked out of the straggling line advancing with a rush on the St. Michiel front and grabbed two Huns who were leading a detachment to a concealed machine gun nest.

"That's nothing," said Rossini. "I could do that any day on Smithfield st." Rossini had previously been wounded at Verdun.

H. C. Swift of Archbald, Pa., was wounded in the neck and shoulder at Soissons, and said he only hoped it wouldn't keep him out of his job at home.

Vennucci's partner, Rossini

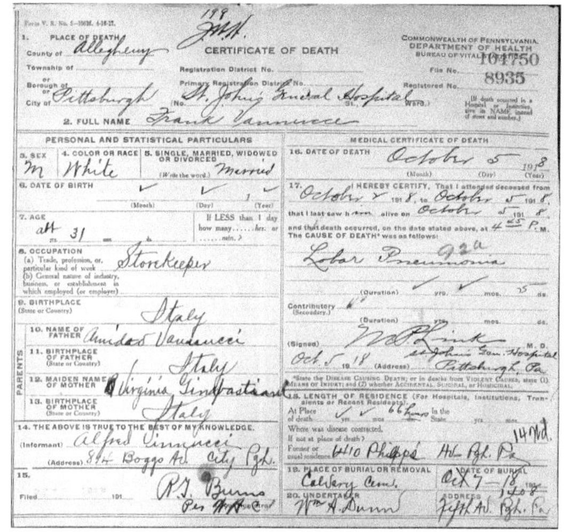

CERTIFICATE OF DEATH

COMMONWEALTH OF PENNSYLVANIA
DEPARTMENT OF HEALTH
BUREAU OF VITAL STATISTICS

File No. 104750
Registered No. 8935

1. PLACE OF DEATH
County of Allegheny
City of Pittsburgh — St. John's General Hospital

2. FULL NAME Frank Vannucci

PERSONAL AND STATISTICAL PARTICULARS

3. SEX M
4. COLOR OR RACE White
5. SINGLE, MARRIED, WIDOWED OR DIVORCED Married
6. DATE OF BIRTH
7. AGE abt 31 yrs.
8. OCCUPATION Storekeeper
9. BIRTHPLACE Italy
10. NAME OF FATHER Amidas Vanducci
11. BIRTHPLACE OF FATHER Italy
12. MAIDEN NAME OF MOTHER Virginia Ginfastiani
13. BIRTHPLACE OF MOTHER Italy
14. THE ABOVE IS TRUE TO THE BEST OF MY KNOWLEDGE.
(Informant) Alfred Vannucci
(Address) 844 Boggs Av. City Pgh.
15. Filed R. J. Burns

MEDICAL CERTIFICATE OF DEATH

16. DATE OF DEATH October 5 1918
17. I HEREBY CERTIFY, That I attended deceased from October 2 1918, to October 5 1918, that I last saw h— alive on October 5 1918, and that death occurred, on the date stated above, at 4.25 P.M. The CAUSE OF DEATH was as follows: Lobar Pneumonia
(Duration) 5 ds.
(Signed) M. D. — St. John's Gen. Hospital, Pittsburgh, Pa.
Oct. 5 1918
18. LENGTH OF RESIDENCE At Place of death 66 hours
Former or usual residence 6410 Phillips Av. Pgh. Pa.
19. PLACE OF BURIAL OR REMOVAL Calvary Cem. DATE OF BURIAL Oct 7 — 18
20. UNDERTAKER Wm A. Dunn ADDRESS 1408 Fifth Av. Pgh. Pa.

Death Certificate, Frank Vennucci

Pale Moon Dealers, Paterni, 5802 Forbes

Jimmy DeLallo—Back in the Day

"When my dad, John DeLallo, bought The Squirrel Hill Cafe in 1976, he said, 'You two (my brother David and I) are going to run it.' We were available and split the workload until 1981, when Ronnie came on board and I went back to school to become a teacher. We showed Ronnie the ropes—all the wisdom we had garnered in two years, what seemed to work.

"David stayed another year to help Ronnie get his foot in the door, so to speak. I don't know the exact arrangement that my dad had with Ronnie, but Ronnie paid his dues; God bless him. The place was rock-solid established and kind of ran itself (we didn't have to promote/advertise (never put an ad in the paper), but that didn't make it easy. People came in forever and stayed forever (not always the best thing). The legacy of the place spoke for itself. We can't take credit for that—a perpetual crazy phenomenon that never stopped—it's still happening.

"Me? I just jumped on in there. I did everything: cooked, bartended, cleaned. We had two shifts—5 am to 6 pm and 6 pm to 2 am—and we switched off days and nights until Ronnie took the helm.

"To be honest (and I think this is still true), The Cage drew a million remarkable people and a million remarkable assholes; it kind of came with the territory. What I remember? The mailmen were funny and I got a kick out of them. But really, it was the sheer number of customers, and we interacted with them all: professors, engineers, lawyers, would-be writers from every generation. It was different every day—the nuances of the characters and their lives. It got me used to city life.

"I don't think that I contributed much, but I showed up for four years. Ronnie was there forever—30 years, I bet. His virtues should be extolled. He was a good businessman and rarely screwed up. And if he did, well, he fixed it. His somewhat gruff (but kind) personality rubbed off the place. It was part of the ambiance, if you can call it that.

Ronnie and I were close, but there was geographical distance between us. I have been in New England for the greater part of my life. When Ronnie died, I knew I would miss him dearly—and I do.

"My mom used to make quilts by hand, so one year, we all pitched in to get Ronnie a Christmas quilt made by our mom. One of the patches is The Squirrel Hill Cafe. I would venture to say that it is a collector's item now. It's a beauty and it reminds me of the amazing people I met and the incredible experience I had, if only for a short time, being part of an institution that Ronnie would make a legend. "

Family-owned DeLallo's Market, Jeanette, PA, where Ronnie bought most of his ingredients, 2020

Hi Jan,

I hope you are well. My brother Jim said you were writing a book/story about the Squirrel Hill Cafe. That is exciting. I don't have any input, just fond memories growing up and my dad taking me there to do accounting work with Mr. George Sodini, the owner prior to my dad. He was a sweet Italian man (friend) of my father's. I would like to hear about it when you have completed it.

Wishing you well.

Chris (Christine DeLallo)

DeLallo's Restaurant, Pittsburgh, PA, owned by Ronnie's brother, Dave DeLallo

Ronnie

Ronnie was both a one-of-a-kind enigma and a stereotypical Italian bachelor. Short and a bit stocky with a balding head and bushy mustache, he smoked and laughed like a fiend. Blunt and a bit crass, you always knew where you stood with Ronnie. He didn't take shit and called it as he saw it, his right eyebrow raised in discreet recognition, like he was always in on the joke.

Ronnie was also kind, funny and warm. He was not above hugging. He was eerily perceptive. He kept an eye on everything, standing at the end of the bar with a smoke hanging from his lips; you could watch his face twitch as he caught something slightly askew out the windows and then moved in to get a closer look

He was protective, but a bit of a scoundrel when it came to women. Though he loved to drink, he never drank on the job or even stayed after for a shot. He came in at 6 a.m. sharp, made his famous Italian sauces and meatballs, his wedding soup, his daily specials and kept an eye on inventory and waste. He was a penny-pincher in the best way. And, he always looked like he was up to something …

Ronnie DeLallo did not live here, go to high school here or knew people here when he bought the Squirrel Hill Cafe.

But, by the time he died decades later, he was as much a pillar of Squirrel Hill as Henry Frick.

It was his joy for life that created the cross-cultural diversification we now call The Cage. Anyone could be there at any given time, from partners at the J. Edson Law Firm to the janitor from the library across the street.

Ron personified an open-mindedness and true liberalness that makes the Squirrel Cage a demilitarized zone from the middle-class capicola restaurants where the staff wears a uniform and serves the same pre-manufactured food with the same pre-manufactured smile day after day. Ron knew all the regulars' names, ordered all food, and cooked all the meals; he was his own security.

The Cage is the only place where I could congratulate the owner for having the best capicola sandwich in Squirrel Hill or a place where the staff would steer me away from dating the wrong woman.

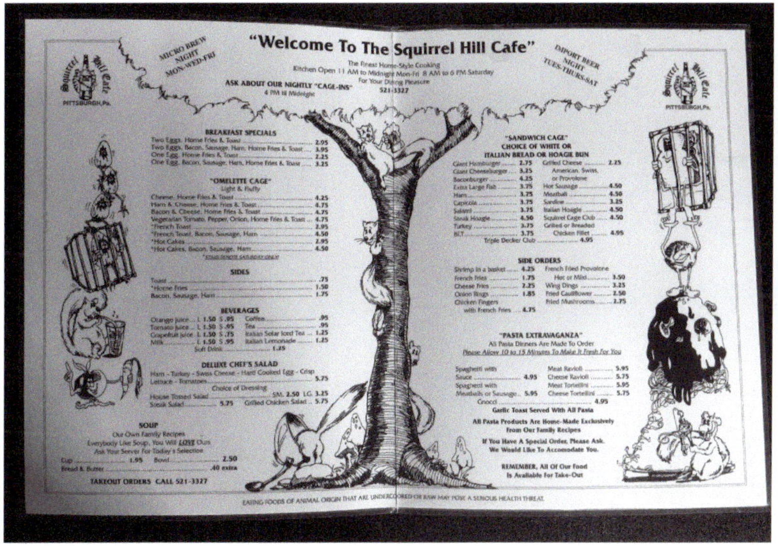

Ronnie, Leslie, Suzie (waitress) & Jeff, Suzie's husband, Seven Springs Bar Competition, circa 1988?

Ronnie would show his gratitude to "his Squirrel Hill" every year by preparing a 6-course Thanksgiving meal, complete with stuffing, pumpkin pie, and cranberry.

The neighborhood needs another Ronnie DeLallo.—***Anonymous***

"I was working the day Ronnie died," recalls Jan. "I heard that he woke up New Year's Day with yellow skin—literally yellow. So, he went to the hospital. I finally saw him after his hospital stay at his home. It was David DeLallo who called to tell me Ronnie died on May 17, 2004. It's strange; that's the same day my mother Florence died.

"Ronnie was a hound dog—loved his women. He chased them. There was one pretty, dark-haired girl who broke his heart. He loved her. He also loved to drink.

Typical male. But, still, he was a human being. He was fair and had values. In the long run, Ronnie wanted to open up a sandwich bar in Arizona, but ended up just buying a place there. He loved Arizona. It's where he went to golf and wanted to finish out his days.

Ronnie came from a family of 11 and learned to cook from his mom. DeLallo's is still a big Italian store in Jeanette. Ronnie used a lot of products from there. Premium stuff. In fact, when Jan and I made our first road trip, we stopped at a place that was selling DeLallo's products. They are everywhere in the region. And, for good reason: authentic Italian.

"I didn't know Ronnie put word out about the bar being for sale," says Jan. When I asked him, he just said, 'yeah.' He died in May and Patty and Rod took over in August.

"A lot of things are different now. We used to have specials every day that Ronnie cooked, and served breakfast the whole time we were open. Obviously, things have changed in Squirrel Hill and there's a lot more competition. People want variety. But people still want great bar food, so we've held our own.

"We still have fresh meatballs and hot sausage, fried fish and burgers. People still love the grilled cheese and egg sandwiches. Wing nights are really popular and we have salads, grilled chicken, fresh-cut fries and coleslaw. Our ½ sandwich and soup for $4.95 is a draw—a really big bargain for the homemade quality. Where can you find a fabulous lunch for $5?"

It was Ronnie DeLallo that gave The Cage its character—its unaffected ambiance, its smoke-and-shot bravado, its neighborly charm, its unadorned appetite, its welcoming air, its hard-ass work ethic, its eternally broken toilets.

I used to joke that I would never quit The Cage before Ronnie fixed the chain on the women's toilet, which, for years was held together by a string of rusting paper clips, but I didn't make it. When it came to persistence, endurance or more aptly, stubbornness, Ronnie always won.

I met Ron DeLallo in the early 70s when I became his plumber. I would often go in early to make repairs. He would be making an enormous pot of soup for lunch. Everyone loved his soup and he loved to make it. He always offered me something to eat. He was happy, even in the morning. Ron made it easy to work for him.

He would put chairs out on the street early in the morning so I had a place to park and unload my tools. When I was alone, he would help me carry big tools and big torches into the cafe. One time, we slid a hot water heater down the front steps in the sidewalk. No job was too big or too little for him to pitch in and help.

If someone didn't show up, Ron would do whatever needed done: cleaning, cooking, setting up. He was always in motion. Sometimes he would run to the bank while I was working, saying, "Don't let anyone in; it's too early for beer!" When there was a plumbing emergency at noon, some of my other plumbing customers would be eating there. They'd say things like, "Hey, Ron, what's my plumber doing here? Make sure you pay him!" Everyone would laugh. Everyone loved Ron's cheerful personality. He laughed, he smiled, he kidded around.

Ron DeLallo was my friend. He made The Cage what it was and what it still is, not just a restaurant, but a collection of friends.

—Albert Sciulli

Jim (We don't Even Know His Last Name)

Everybody remembers Jim. We have no idea when he started, but it was after Freddie. Jim was a cook—a good cook. He was a thin, black man with a wicked but charming grin, a crooked laugh and an evil streak when he was crossed. One time, Jan and Jim didn't talk for six weeks—a hard battle in such a small room. She had no idea what had happened, why.

"I would give him food orders and he would give me my food. Not a word spoken. It's a confined workspace and if one thing is off, it can mess up the whole thing—the whole dynamics of the place. Jim was a proud man—proud of his food—and didn't take shit. It's one of the best ways to survive in that room."

Finally, Jan broke the ice and asked if she did something wrong. He said, "I thought you were mad at me." And so The Cage turns. They laughed and got back to work.

"Once Jim put a curse on me," says Leslie. "I knew he had some Cajun thing going on and was afraid there was a dead rooster involved. He wouldn't speak to me and made an obvious show of turning his back—especially when I needed food. He took his good old time. Finally, I asked Jim what was wrong. I don't remember what he said (again, who should be writing a memoir if they don't remember), only that he lifted the curse and everything was fine from there on out.

"I attended his funeral with Danny Morrow and cried. You would think I would know his last name. Maybe he wasn't meant to have one. Such a singular man with a deep and shadowed soul.

Maybe 'Jim' was enough. Why he was working at The Cage I will never know. But he was a good cook.

You just wanted to stay on his good-cook side."

JC—A Soft Wild

Jan first met JC when he was tending bar at the Derby in Regent Square. His wife, Treva, was pregnant with her first child, a son they named Catan. Catan is a North Dakota Indian name that means the 4th born is a male child. JC had three previous daughters who lived with his ex-wife in Florida. Catan was born with Down's Syndrome.

A used car salesman once said he never went to the Derby unless he was packing. The owner did a "little" remodeling and renamed it Charlie's 10¢ Saloon. However, the rough atmosphere of the bar never changed. The owner, Charlie, was one of the worst violent offenders, so it's been said.

JC wasn't a large man, but he was a "Crazy Indian" with long, white hair, who was able to control most of the bar violence unless someone aroused his temper.

After a few years, JC left the Saloon and divorced Treva. They agreed upon joint custody with JC staying home with Catan most of the time. As Catan got older, JC took a job at The Cage as a cook. He frequently brought Catan to The Cage when he was off work, which Treva didn't necessarily agree with, but admits it added to Catan's ability to socialize and be comfortable when out and about.

In 2012, JC had a double stroke and went from the hospital to a nursing home. It was strange to see such a large and vivacious man needing any kind of care at all. Treva took Catan to see his father 2-3 times a week for nearly two years until JC passed. JC wanted to be cremated and his urn sits on Catan's dresser.

Catan and Treva have made their way. Catan has worked part-time as a bagger at the Shadyside Giant Eagle for 11 years now—a full life, including amazing parents. These stories are also a huge part of The Cage continuum. Everyone who walks through that door.

Brenda & Melissa

Jim DeLuca & Friend

Jay & Zach, Beer Guys

Ron Costello

Chip

Everything Settles at the Bottom

"Lunches at The Cage were crazy in the 1980s," says Jan. "There were so many businesses in Squirrel Hill with workers who had only a half-hour for lunch. From 11:30 am to 1 pm, everyone worked together, all trying to turn tables over as quick and appetizingly as we could. We had one bartender, one cook (sometimes he was working on 6 checks at a time), one dishwasher, one prep person and two waitresses. It was madness, but we became veterans of the lunch rush and could turn the tables over three times in an hour. Nothing could shake us.

"Our shifts lasted until 6 o'clock, so we had to deal with happy hour, too. From 4 p.m. to 6 p.m. Iron drafts were 25¢ and we served peanuts in the shell for free at the bar. Talk about a mess! The clean-up was awful 'cause people would step on them. Made me crazy. And you could get drunk on $1.50. But lots of people came in and the booths were always full.

"Even though we weren't open for breakfast, you could get breakfast all day long: omelets, French toast, pancakes, home fries and toast. You'd be surprised how many omelets I served at happy hour."

Everyone agreed that Ronnie DeLallo was a fabulous cook. He was a chef in the military, feeding 100s of hungry soldiers, and before that, a student of his mother, who taught him Italian cuisine, both hearty and refined. He made homemade dishes every day at the break of dawn, from soups to sauces to the daily special. He made a different soup every weekday of the month, but was renowned throughout Pittsburgh for his wedding soup—rich and savory with those tiny homemade meatballs. "I have never tasted anything like it and never will again," remembers Jan, "I wish we still had the recipe.

"When I think about the most outstanding dishes, I remember Ronnie's Italian Braciole (stuffed steak), his lasagna, sausage, and, of course, spaghetti and meatballs. Plus, the fresh salads were always made with real greens before it was cool (leaf lettuce, complete with the occasional grit of the real dirt it came from, despite being washed and dried), the best grilled cheese in the city and fried cheese balls that are famous to this day. Our fried egg and sardine sandwiches were big, too. We no longer serve sardines, but ask for a

couple of hard-boiled eggs and hot sauce and you're good to go!

The burgers here have saved my life more than once. —Stephen Tallam

---

"Everything was Ronnie's way. He taught me portion control—never too many meatballs. He definitely knew how to run a business. Like when Theresa, his sister, used to make desserts—I remember the Amaretto Ricotta Cheese Pie. The staff loved it so much, we ate it all. Finally, Ronnie made us pay; we were eating the profits."

"Stir the soup" was his daily chant. Everything settles at the bottom.

Wings

Cage Club

Famous Hot Balls

---

*If you have time to lean, you have time to clean.—**Ronnie DeLallo***

The Landscape, Circa 1980

At the time both Jan and I began work, Squirrel Hill was much different than it is today: still bustling and lively, but with a singular character. Not that it isn't magic now, but it was free from the contemporary chain-store numbness of Dunkin' Donuts, Starbucks, Rita's Italian Ice, Rite Aid, PNC Bank and the like.

The stores and restaurants were independently owned and sui generis. Let's paint a streetscape: the fabled Waldorf Bakery that lured people from far and wide; both the Squirrel Hill and Atlantic bookstores—the epitome of the independent bookstore haven; O'Rourke's Bar, where live music was a thing; The Pussycat lingerie (ooh la la); The Bagel Nosh, where you could get a Bloody Mary at breakfast and the best authentic Jewish bagels in the city; Sir Loin, where seniors ate cheap from 4 p.m. to 6 p.m.; Adele's & Linton's where you could buy designer women's clothes; Newman's Children's store, where many a private school uniform was purchased.

My first encounter with Squirrel Hill was in 1966 when I was 13 and a classmate's family moved to Douglas Street. I would spend weekends there and loved that Squirrel Hill had such a wonderful, lively business district unlike Bethel Park, where I lived. Later, I worked for the National Record Mart and a co-worker was transferred to the Squirrel Hill branch. After work we would go to the Sir Loin for beers and from there to the Squirrel Hill Cafe. I loved the atmosphere there as well as the music. That was in the early 1980s.

Years later, after living in New York City and then Dormont, I took an apartment on Darlington Road. I popped in again one night to The Cage and bingo! I felt right at home with the atmosphere, music, customers and staff. It was just like being in a bar on Bleecker Street in Greenwich Village, only Pittsburgh style. I lived there for seven years and became friends with many customers and the various staff members… Jan, Billy, Matt, John, Ben behind the bar; Caitlin and Chrissie who were servers; and so many of the regular customers that space forbids me from listing them all. I still stop in once in a while and am glad it is all still the same. Hope it never changes!

—Ron Miller

Forbes & Murray Ave., 1965?

Then, there was the London Dock and Coach House (equally expensive clothes for men); Rosen's Drugstore; Walden Flowers; Isaly's Ice Cream; Heads Together (a local head shop with bongs and paraphernalia, used books and later, video rentals with a back XXX room); The Record Rubble for used albums and CDs; the Personality Beauty Shop; Liberty Travel Agency; Oliver's Flowers; The Camera Store; The National Record Mart; Sun Drug; Rhoda's, famous for their authentic Reuben sandwiches, and the list goes on and on ...

Some persevered: The Squirrel Hill Newsstand; Murray Avenue Grill; Footers Cleaners; the aforementioned Little's Shoes; S.W, Randall Toyes & Gifts (yes, they spell toys with an "e"); Pamela's Diner, renowned for their pancakes; The Manor Theatre; Mineo's, Napoli's and Aiello's Pizza (pizza seems to have a stronghold against evolution); and the Framesmith; where Billy the bartender worked before securing his place as a Cage institution, all remain vital.

But it is not the same. Nothing is ever the same. Still, change is good, right? We now have a Bruegger's Bagels; lots of nice coffee shops; The Exchange with used CDs and DVDs; Ten Thousand Villages; Everyday Noodles; Avalon Exchange (cool resale clothing); plus, restaurants like Aladdin's; locally owned Independent Brewing Company; the upscale Bangkok Balcony; and Paititi Inti, an authentic Peruvian fashion store. We even have a Farmer's Market down on Murray each Sunday in the summer.

Once a primarily a Jewish neighborhood, the demographic is now much more mixed, and unfortunately, the character somehow muted. Still home to many synagogues, one Jewish restaurant and one Jewish market, Squirrel Hill isn't the same—did we mention that?

One thing that hasn't changed much is the Squirrel Hill Cafe. And that's exactly why it is a Pittsburgh legend and why, in 2017, Chef Anthony Bourdain included it in his feature on Pittsburgh.

I was a regular at the Cage from 1996-2006, while I was a grad student at CMU. I loved that I could come in at any time, day or night, sit at the bar and strike up a conversation with someone from just about any walk of life—a retired steelworker, a professor, a guy who worked at the Photoshop up Murray or a woman getting off her Giant Eagle shift. Everybody came into The Cage.

Most often I came in the evenings, alone or with friends, and almost always would run into more friends. We'd sit in the booths for hours-long bull sessions or collect around the pinball machine. I wrote most of my qualifying exams in the back booth. Technically I met my husband at the 61C Café, but our romance blossomed here.

This is a place where the staff makes you feel like family. All the way from the top—Ronnie himself and long-timers like Jan and Billy, Chireen, Don, to servers who came and went... and came back again, like the Coyne sisters—everyone made us feel at home. I remember once, about five years after I moved away to take a job, coming back for a visit and walking into The Cage. Jan was behind the bar. She greeted me nonchalantly with my usual order—"Pint of Pabst and a grilled cheese?" As if I had never left. It made my whole year!

—***Courtney Maloney***

Food, Fame & Anthony Bourdain

Imagine the excitement when we learned that we were to be featured in Anthony Bourdain's *Pittsburgh: Parts Unknown* (although we would personally argue that The Cage is very well known).

It was June 8, 2017 when Bourdain sat with author and friend Stewart O'Nan and had a conversation filmed at The Cage. They talked about the steel industry, Pittsburgh's transition from blue collar to white collar, a loss of population in the 80s, our current medical and technological triumph—and Pittsburgh's affordability.

The Cage was here through all of that, but not a word was said about its contribution to the historical culinary bar food tradition of Pittsburgh, which was disappointing overall—we naively thought they were going to talk about the burgers, the drinks, the atmosphere, the goddamn hot balls, but The Cage was merely a stage for the conversation.

Jan with Bourdain film crew

I think we all missed the fact that this was not a food show so much as an historical perspective of Pittsburgh—old & new—which took us, in the end, to wrestling, which none of us Pittsburgh natives knew was a thing. My theory is that Bourdain was paying tribute to Pittsburgh's renowned obsession with sports, but felt he had to uncover something. Bourdain labeled wrestling "the greatest show on earth," but I don't think any of them (the wrestlers or the fans) eat at The Cage. And what about the Greatest Burger on Earth? We deserved a little MVP status.

Today, the chair that Anthony Bourdain sat in at The Cage in is marked so customers can feel a little closer to this culinary hero when they come in for a little respite.

"We are proud to be part of a celebrated man's contribution to the grittier, real side of American dining and great food, if only as a backdrop," said Carly Albert, the then Kitchen Manager at The Cage, who claims that Bourdain's *Kitchen Confidential* informed her life and approach to being a Chef. "We feel honored that he came by."

You can watch the episode in full here: https://www.dailymotion.com/video/x6mtvr3.

Jan, Kelli, Billy, Chrisy, Dan Tom, Anthony, Alex, Tina, Matt

I was lucky enough to film at The Cage for an episode of CNN's "Anthony Bourdain: Parts Unknown." I'm a producer for the series, and we filmed a scene there with Tony and local author Stewart O'Nan. After talking with Jan and having a few beers and burgers, The Cage became one of my favorites in Pittsburgh.

Thanks,

Josh Ferrell

Stewart O'Nan—Town & Gown

While I grew up in Point Breeze and spent much of my teenage years in Squirrel Hill, I was more of a regular at the Squirrel Hill Newsstand right next door, reading the new comic books every Tuesday, and the Isaly's next to it. And, I was always at the library across the street, which was brand new at the time. Strange that I never ran into the teen-aged Michael Chabon back then. Later we'd both play the Electric Banana—a weird bit of literary trivia.

I left Pittsburgh in 1979, and while I came back every year to visit family, the only times I went to The Cage was when I was reading at Pitt or CMU, Duquesne or Chatham. Along with Chuck Kinder and Diane's place on Wightman Street, and Hemingway's in Oakland, it was one of literary Pittsburgh's favorite watering holes, hospitable to grad students. The food was cheap, the booths were cozy and you could smoke, plus I liked how the neon looked with the lights down low, and they'd probably have the Pens or Pirates game on for the regulars.

The Cage has always seemed a happy mix of town and gown, young and old, so when Anthony Bourdain's production staff asked me where he could interview me about how Pittsburgh's changed, it seemed a natural setting—not really a dive at all, but a place where everyone's welcome, except Raiders and Ravens fans.

Chris Schmidt & his famous Cage painting (prints available for sale at the bar)

Every Day's a Holiday at The Cage

Well, that's not really true, but you can bet anytime you go in, somebody is celebrating something.

Halloween

Halloween is a huge deal at the bar. Tina and Chrisy decorate from top to bottom, including stupid amounts of cobwebs. We host a costume contest and of course, have a wide variety of craft pumpkin beers, which people can't seem to get enough of. It is a night when everyone feels free to be their other selves.

Doodle, Ethan Stang, R.I.P.

Vampires and witches, princesses and pirates, Shakespeare and Satan, everyone looking to celebrate the macabre comes to The Cage—the most enthusiastic Halloween hosts in town. And, of course, we all dress up, too!

It was St. Patty's day, 2012. I had just finished my shift at the Commonplace Coffee Shop across the street. I remember it was unseasonably warm that year and I was drenched in sweat. I was fairly new to Pittsburgh and my coworker, Sarah, came in to invite me to The Cage for the Dirty Limerick Contest. I remember getting the last two seats at the bar, and the AC cooled my aching body. The jokes were funny, the pints were cold, the crowd was lively, and we had the best time. I've been coming here now for six years and I can't thank the staff enough—Jan, Billy, Tina, Matt, John—and everyone else. Thank you for taking care of this place and allowing us all to come in and be a part of it, even just for a little while.

—Dan Drummond

Thanksgiving

Then there is Thanksgiving. Back in the day, Ronnie would cook a traditional feast and not just serve it, but take to-go orders. It was crazy. Customers had to order two weeks in advance just to get it. And, the anticipation was palpable. He made fresh-roasted turkey, real mashed potatoes, baked yams, corn, acorn squash soup, cranberry sauce.

OK, admittedly, he sent Jan to pick up 12-15 pumpkin pies from Giant Eagle, but he topped them with real whipped cream and made everything very affordable, although he was a penny-pincher. Customers swarmed in for lunch the whole Thanksgiving week and to-go orders went flying out of the door. For some people, this *was* their Thanksgiving Dinner and Ronnie knew that.

Christmas

Christmas is another Cage classic. The jolly just get jollier and the generosity of patrons and staff rises to a lovely Dickensesque pinnacle.

Circa 1980: Back: Terry, Dave & Jimmy DeLallo, unknown. Front: Erin, Judy, Jan, Carol, Rose and the middle-ish people there are also a mystery.

Customers come home for the holiday and make special plans to meet loved ones, happy-hour-ers exchange gifts, carols ring full-tilt on the juke-box, glasses clink, drinks are shared and Jan plays Santa Claus with a bag of gifts for all of her regulars. Even the Scroogiest of Scrooges can't resist the allure of a drink, a smile, a cheer and a toast to feeling of family, fun, festivity, a garland and a garnish.

The Cage was my hangout place through the 80s and mid 90s.One of my favorite memories of the Cage is when I would come in and Jim, the cook, would ask if I wanted MY salad. He would make a wonderful salad, always adding some extra pepperoncini and an extra hard-boiled egg for me. Being there in the atmosphere of the Cage made it the best salad ever.

Also, during the holidays I would bake a selection of cookies. Then, a couple of hours before Ronnie closed for Christmas, I would bring in a tray and we would sit around with whoever was there—staff and customers—and celebrate the joy of being together, sharing a drink and wishing everyone a Merry Christmas. Fond, fond memories of a place I still consider the best bar in Pittsburgh.

—Jeanne Scardamalia

The Best Windows in the City of Pittsburgh

Many theories/myths exist about how the Squirrel Hill Cafe became known as "The Cage." Almost all of them come down to the windows that originally were smaller panes separated by vertical and horizontal rims that formed a cage-like impression. Why they were changed? Many stories exist about that, too, from practical heating bills to a fight that broke out and smashed one of the panes forcing replacement. We'll never know, but The Cage windows still serve their purpose.

"I am nebby, as we say here in Pittsburgh," admits Jan. "I love to know and see what's going on. That's why our windows that look right out onto the corner of Forbes and Murray have always been like a movie to me—a soap opera. You see everything. People kissing, people fighting, people so busy on their phones that they walk into the pole. The people who race across the street trying to beat the light (go on green, never in-between). You can't find a better perch on the world. Just ask the regulars who claim those window seats as their own every day for lunch and happy hour. You sit there and you don't miss a thing.

"In general, I just like watching people—seeing what they wear and how they act. I've seen styles change over the years, you know from all the big hair and big shoulder pads then all the ripped stuff. Now, all the hair colors. Crazy. Women come by with like 6-8 kids in strollers and I wonder about their stories. Then, there's all the jerks that park in the no-parking zone right in front of the bar so our beer vendors can't deliver, the people that just sit down and start playing music for money across the street, the beggars and, yes, the drunks (they don't come from our place).

"There's the annual Vintage Grand Prix at Schenley Park. And, for three or four days, all these old fancy cars drive up and down Forbes Ave. It's like you went back in time or something. And there's the dogs, so many dogs, so many different kinds. Oh, and the women walking around in bras and slippers. At first, I was shocked. Now, not so much. You can't imagine what I've seen through those windows. You couldn't make this stuff up.

"A few winters ago, during what is now known as the Snowpocalypse in Pittsburgh, we got like two feet of snow, I was working (yes, we were still open) and happened to look over at the church caddy-corner from the bar and there was a young girl standing by the church sign making a snow sculpture: a life-sized snow penis with balls at the base. A cop stopped

and the girl ran. He ran across the street, up the hill, fell, and then got up and kicked the snow penis down. That's a perfect day at The Cage.

"Then, there's the annual street fair—Squirrel Hill Happening—when they used to have a petting zoo over in the church yard. You could watch goats and rabbits all day. The street is closed off, so it is full of pedestrians—shoppers—and it's always a mess of hair colors and clothes and make-up and the expressions on people's faces. I could watch all day.

"Every once in a while, I hear a bunch of motorcycles coming up Forbes—the grind, the rumble—I love that sound, but that's just me.

"I particularly like it when I see older people walking by and holding hands; it makes me feel good. There are the men with babies—you see lots more of that now. Once I saw a woman in a wheelchair pushing a stroller. Made me pause to think about what kind of life she must lead. I guess that's the thing. What you see through the windows is both ordinary and extraordinary. You can't help but think about other people.

Then, of course, there are the assholes that go through the lights, putting mascara on and texting. I want them to know, I see you—it's an accident waiting to happen. I've often dreamed of having the time to videotape them and report them. It makes me angry, but there's not much I can do.

"The biggest thing over the years is phones. People are so focused on their phones that I feel like they are missing everything I see and some things they should see. They are missing out on what it means to be walking around Squirrel Hill—the sights, the sounds. And sometimes they are just stupid, not paying attention to their kids or the lights.

"Mostly I want to say, 'Mothers please, stop texting and hold your little ones' hands.' The intersection at Forbes and Murray is dangerous. It's a matter of time before someone gets killed at that corner. Cars go through the walk sign and red light. Sometimes I close my eyes."

Pure Evil, Saturday, October 27, 2018

"I was at work that Saturday morning, looking out the windows as I do; it was going on 10 a.m.

"It's not that unusual to see a police car fly by, maybe two, but then there were more and more coming up Murray, then an ambulance, a second and a third. They were all headed toward Wilkins Avenue. They were flying and just kept coming. I thought there must be a bad accident … but then I saw a SWAT team, then another. I turned on the news. Then my daughter Amy called. Then, my daughter-in-law, Suzanne, called from the hospital because her parents had called her…

"As people were praying and celebrating at The Tree of Life Synagogue on Shady Avenue, evil walked through the door with hell in its pocket.

"There are shootings every day in Pittsburgh, but when you know a person who has been shot and killed, it's very

different. I knew Danny Stein—actually, I knew Danny's wife Sharon—who would come in for lunch when she worked at the Jewish Community Center a couple of doors down. She, Diane and Nancy were regulars for a couple of years. I only saw Danny from time to time at family gatherings: he was my son-in-law's uncle. Pittsburgh is close that way.

"By the time I left work that black evening, a sea of people had gathered at the corner of Forbes and Murray. I knew that Danny had been murdered and that this sea was a wave of mourning. I passed through it feeling both the push and the pull, the warmth and the fear, the sorrow and the coming together, the anger and the truth.

"Danny & Sharon have a daughter, Lee, and a son, Joey. They have a grandchild: little Henry. I know Danny is in the sunshine now. I know there is a black cloud over Squirrel Hill. I know this has to stop."

STEIN
DANIEL A.
Age 71, of Squirrel Hill, On Saturday, October 27, 2018. Beloved husband of Sharyn; loving father of Joseph (Jeannina) and Leigh Stein; devoted grandfather of Henri Federico Stein; much loved brother of Ruth Halle; son of the late Bernard and Yetta Stein; brother-in-law of Faye and the late Joseph Konigsberg; many, many loving family and friends. Dan was a past President of New Light Congregation and current President of their Men's Club. Funeral and interment private. Professional services trusted to the **D'ALESSANDRO FUNERAL HOME & CREMATORY, LTD.**, Lawrenceville. Memorial contributions may be made to the Crohn's and Colitis Foundation or the Squirrel Hill Food Pantry.
www.dalessandroltd.com
Send condolences post-gazette.com/gb

The Current Cage Crew

Night server, Ariel, 2020

2017 Cage Crew

Lamar, Day Cook, 2020

Billy the Bartender

March, 1986–present (excepting August 2005-January, 2007)

It's been a long time since Billy and I got together. This book was the perfect excuse to catch up, so over the Christmas holiday we found an evening for a little wine and cheese, which translates into Tito's and Boursin.

What I always find beautiful about Billy is how comfortable he is in his own skin. He is known throughout the city for his beard, which he swears he won't shave until he is completely out of debt. A long-time smoker (he still lights everyone's cigarette at the bar), Billy now vapes. His smile comes easy, as does his laugh.

When I (Leslie) started at The Cage somewhere in the mid-eighties, I remember Billy being there; he thinks he came later. He remembers I was already there. I feel like I always was there, so he may be right. He has more history than I. So, we'll say Billy started at The Cage in 1986, right around when I started.

"I went to bartending school before I was old enough to drink," says Bill. "Then, I worked at a truck stop between New Castle and Butler, PA. It was in the middle of the sticks and mostly what I remember is picking myself up off of the bar floor after some stupid bar fight. I was living in Ellwood City where I grew up. The bar had bands on the weekend. It was a tough place. Drunks. Fights. Not a good scene.

"Unfortunately, in the end, it made me not want to tend bar anymore, so I worked some sales jobs selling vacuum cleaners (I know, right?) and I took a job in Greentree essentially selling shit out of a bag. That's what brought me to Pittsburgh. The Ellwood commute was too much and I was going through cars left and right.

"Finally, I got an apartment in Squirrel Hill with a buddy, Charlie, who worked with me. We sold knives, car stereos, cheap speakers, random shit—and it was all on commission. We had to sell it or pay for it. I did this from the time I was 19-20 or so. Charlie got a job working in a parking garage downtown and ended up building parking garages and did well.

"After we got the apartment, I got a job working at Framesmith on Forbes, but it was minimum wage. I was kind of down. Charlie said, "You need to get the hell out of the house." He recommended The Cage. They had 25¢ drafts on Friday. 'It won't cost you anything,' he said. I folded. I went up there and sat at one of the front tables. Jan waited on me. I had a couple of beers, chilled and chatted with Jan, who was waitressing then. I asked her, "You looking for a bartender?" knowing full well it was a slim chance. Jan said, "The owner, Ronnie, is tending bar right now." He was tending bar because he just fired Big John, but that's another story). I talked to him and introduced myself.

"Ronnie asked if I was working, if I had tended bar before and if I had references. 'Leave me your name and phone number,' he said. He didn't want a resume. I didn't think anything of it, but ends up, he called and talked to Ed (my boss) at the Framesmith; made sure I wasn't lying. Then, a week later, he called me and offered me the job: Monday, Wednesday and Friday day shift.

"It was busy. I was overwhelmed constantly. Daytime lunches were a crunch—over $900 in sales. Compared to working at the truck stop, it was great. Fridays were simply insane. I did that for about six months. Then he fired somebody else: Big Mike, and I started working nights. Everyone was 'big.'

"Mostly The Cage is a comfortable place where you can get to know people. It's not always the same crowd, changes over the years, particularly late night. Every year, there are newbies; it keeps it fresh. No, I don't like going to work. But once I get there, I like being there—a lot more than I can say about many jobs I worked. You get to meet/talk with everyone. Every shift is a new experience.

"Back in the day, Ronnie made everything from scratch and served really good meat. You know me. I have a hard time making peanut butter & jelly, so I'm pretty happy with anything. But, I love the burgers. Usually I don't eat until 4 or 5 in the morning, but the cooks hook me up. They make me a huge Chef's salad or a grilled chicken salad that I eat after work—tons of meat and cheese. Let's just say I'm not starving. When I get off early on Thursday, I usually get a meatball or hot sausage sandwich. The soups are really good, too.

"I try not to eat deep-fried, but the hot balls are so damn good and the wings are f'in awesome. And, people swear by fish sandwiches. We don't have sardines any more, but we still sell hard-boiled eggs.

"The Cage is a local bar, not especially trendy, even though it's popular with a high amount of traffic. I love it because of the people—we get a little bit of everything—from students to professionals to people that just live in the area. A lot of people come back on the holidays. I only see them once or twice a year—Thanksgiving, Christmas, or when someone is sick—that's not so nice.

What do I look forward to? Maybe crass to say, but it's always nice when I have several good-looking women at the bar—makes the night go a little sweeter. Obviously,

getting restaurant employees makes for a good night. I don't think anything I do is really life changing. Maybe certain things I say affect people, and I certainly talk to enough. Point is, you can randomly say something important. I hope I accidentally do some people some good sometimes."

Billy Nagel, 2020, sans beard

Great $3.00 hamburgers and number one bartender in Pittsburgh: Billy.—John R.

Matt—Not For Everyone

Matt has been a bartender at The Cage for more than 10 years. He is quick to smile and just as quick to cut to the chase. He sees through a lot of crap, but then lets it roll off his back—nature of the beast. Young and articulate with attentive eyes and more than attentive bartending skills, nobody waits long for a drink on his shift and multi-tasking is one of his finest skills. That, and his generous humor.

"How did I end up here? I was good friends with Bill. One night I was walking past to make a night deposit from my job as Bar Manager at Gullifty's (a long-time Squirrel Hill restaurant famous for their desserts, which has since closed) and Bill flagged me in to ask if I was looking for a part-time job. I said, 'Yea, actually. Totally.' Six weeks went by and the next thing I knew I was behind the bar working every Thursday, Friday and Saturday or filling in for Billy when he needed a day off.

"I love and hate this place. Mostly love it. It's authentic and honest. Nobody's trying to trick anyone about what you're getting here. There's no schmooze. And, I make a relatively good living. Good nights can be $350, but we bust our asses.

"All of my closest friends are from here and also a lot of the people I hate to see. It's a dichotomy. But you're going to have that. It's the same when you walk the streets of Squirrel Hill. You know everyone. You kind of can't get away from it."

Originally from Crafton, south of Pittsburgh, Matt has a degree in Creative Writing from the University of Pittsburgh in nonfiction and journalism. "I did a funny thing. I took five years off before I finished my degree, so I was like the 10-year student. I got jaded about the writing program for a while and got a salaried job at Gullifty's, so I was making money, which kind of derailed me from finishing my degree for a while."

Matt met Chrisy when he started working here. They were friends five years before they started dating. Today they are living together and just moved to Wilkinsburg. "I would love to buy a house and stop working weekends, but that's not really in the cards right now," admits Matt with a sigh.

"You have to have a lot of patience to bartend here and I do. People tell me that. I've had to break up fights—usually about a girl—and people can be shitty and do dumb shit. That part's never fun. It's only happened a handful of times in a decade, but you get that adrenaline rush. It's like being a first responder. You have to deal with it with little to no resources. Sometimes I would like to hit someone, but I would never do that. It's a weird responsibility; I hate when that stuff happens.

"But, it's also great not having a boss down your neck. They really trust us here and I don't take that for granted. I also love hanging out with all these guys and getting to know each other. Ask Tina about the dance parties.

"And the Halloween thing is a blast. About three years ago, Chrisy dressed up as a squirrel. Usually we have themed costumes. Sometimes it works out, sometimes not. Last year was classic monsters. Funny thing, everyone makes Bill's costumes for him, so I thought they would make mine. They don't. One year, Tina dressed as a Girl Scout but looked more like a military dictator. It's hilarious.

"But, it's not for everyone. We don't get done until 5 a.m. on Saturday nights sometimes. As employees, we get $1 off everything and we all have tabs at the end of the night. Then we go to Ritter's Diner or Billy's favorite, Eat'n Park, for breakfast. I love being out in the early mornings, but then you sleep until one or two the next day. Did I say it's not for everyone?

Chrisy—The Squirrel Cage Wheel

Why do they call it the Squirrel Cage? I can't tell you how many times I've been asked this question during my time as a waitress here. It certainly isn't a proper Cafe—the coffee is god-awful (I drink the iced tea). I have made up many answers over the years, but really "squirrel cage" is an old term used for what we now call a hamster wheel, the device upon which a rodent runs and runs with no apparent outcome.

I imagine since the dawn of The Cage that this bar has had daily regulars who come in and drink and eat and bullshit and spend their money only to get up the next day, go to work, and do the same thing again once they get off. Same beer, same shot, burger the same way each time—The Cage is definitely a haven for those who take comfort in consistency. All who frequent the bar, especially those who have been patrons for years (or who have left and come back to visit), know that things don't change here. The staff has barely changed in the last ten years, and some of us have been here for decades. In fact, if you were to tell me when I applied for this job ten years ago that I would still be here now, I honestly can't imagine how I'd react.

After ten years of running on the Squirrel Cage wheel, I have poured countless draft beers, served countless cocktails, dumped ashtrays, portioned salad dressing, listened to Hotel California and Bohemian Rhapsody (ugh, please stop with these), stocked booze (yes, this is what we use the dumb waiter for—not to feed the troll in the basement your leftovers or to steal credit card numbers as I have once been accused), answered the same phone call (kitchen closes *at midnight*), cleared empty plates, washed dirty glasses, cut off drunk people, called them cabs, cleaned up their vomit, took out the trash, turned out the lights, and went home for the night countless times. Sometimes I wonder what the hell I am still doing here.

But for all those repetitive tasks, there are a million reasons why I still enjoy working at The Cage. First and foremost, I cannot explain how close of friends I have become to my coworkers past and present. I met the love of my life working at The Cage, as have so many others. Though the late nights are rough, I love having the park, bank, grocery stores, etc. to myself while the 9-5ers are at work, and I haven't set an alarm to wake up for literally years.

I could laugh for the rest of my life thinking about the antics that have occurred in the bar once customers are gone and the door is locked. As a lifelong Pittsburgher, I take pride in working somewhere that feels like "old Pittsburgh" in a time where investors rather than families open restaurants with concepts and menus that mean nothing to anyone. This is not just an indulgence in nostalgia, but feeling proud that we can provide an environment where people feel at home, not just to those who grew up here, but to anyone with whom The Cage resonates.

And because people feel at home, they come to The Cage when they didn't get the job, to tell us they got engaged (in some cases, to get engaged), for their first drink after having a baby, to celebrate birthdays and graduations, when their loved ones have died. I wrote eulogies for my grandmother and my father in a booth at The Cage and have gotten very drunk with my friends in their mourning and my own. I have also gotten very drunk in celebration and also just because.

The last ten years of my life has unfolded with The Cage as a primary recurring scene. Time really does fly when you're having fun. Maybe too much fun.

Thanks to Jan and Leslie for putting together everyone's cherished memories, and cheers to my best friends and coworkers who have shared in my Cage years. I love yinz, Bill, Ariel, Kellie, Alex, Tina, Caitlin, and especially Matt. To many more car bombs together!

Kellie—The Longest Healthy Relationship

It's a Sunday night at The Cage, Matt is working the bar and Kira, the floor. Jan is here with Kellie and Carly so we can chat.

I insist on buying Kellie her beer and tell Matt NOT to let Jan pay for our tab (you can see where this is going). Kellie bums a smoke from Jan and we sit down to talk in a back booth. The place fills up quickly, but we don't notice.

Kellie is a beautiful mix of hope and sadness—just a little bit around the edges. She is 27, tall, smart, careful and attractive. I like the way her eyes light up when she talks about art and writing. I like her honesty and her eyebrows.

"I am the first person to go to college in my family," begins Kellie. "It's kind of a big deal. I got my degree at Pitt Greensburg, a satellite campus, but first applied to Pitt main. I really wanted to be in the city, but my parents convinced me otherwise.

I knew that when I graduated, I would come to Pittsburgh. And, I did.

"I came here with a writing degree (emphasis in nonfiction/personal essay) and $600. I lived with friends, who were doing their masters at Chatham University. Rent was $500 a month. It was nothing to them; it was a lot to me. My parents helped me out a bit in the beginning, but it was hard. I needed to make money.

"I went on dozens of interviews, but my summer college work as a receptionist for Alternative Community Resource Program in Greensburg, ends up, didn't really count as experience. I ended up at Panera, 7 am to 3 pm, 5 days a week making sandwiches and salads on the line. We had to wear uniforms I couldn't afford. So, I was pretty psyched when I found a pair of men's khakis online for $20. They were a little long, but so what. My Manager said I needed to get them hemmed. Hemming, like I can do/afford that. I knew my Panera career was not long for this world."

Kellie shifts a bit, her eyes get a little dreamy. We order another.

"I drew a lot and thought about how I could get into illustrating children's books, but all my friends who had gone to the Art Institute were in the hole, as was I with my school loans. One job was never enough, and then there was healthcare, which I would only have through my parents until I turned 26 … I also thought about writing a graphic memoir. I still might do that.

"I was not a big bar person, but occasionally stopped in The Cage with my laptop, my drawing pad/stylus for a fish sandwich. I would write, draw and watch other people. Sometimes I came with a friend (that was back when I drank PBRs—that ship has sailed. Now I am kind of a craft beer snob).

"Anyway, one night, four years ago this May (2018), I came in and there was a 'Help Wanted' sign. Tina gave me an application and I filled it out. I had no experience serving, so I thought nothing of it. Then, in the 10 minutes walking home from my bus stop, the phone rang. I didn't recognize the number, but answered it anyway. It was Patty asking me for an interview. I felt so lucky.

"I told Panera I had a doctor's appointment and met Patty. Not only did she offer me the job, but she said she liked me. That meant the world to me. (Kellie smiles.) She gave me Thursday nights and every other Saturday. I worked both jobs, trying to save up money. For a while I worked Sunday nights with Billy. They were either dead or insane but they were always fun.

"Truthfully, the longest, healthiest relationship I've ever had is with this place. My coworkers are like family. We communicate and have each other's back. I was scared at first, worried that I wasn't good enough, but I'm glad I did this. It's given me an invaluable sense of ability. And, even my boss at UPMC said that what I've learned in the service industry has informed my work ethic and she totally trusts me to get things done. She even comes in every once in a while ...

"Of course, sometimes I still don't think I know what I am doing. I have nights with customers like, "Fuck you. I work harder than you. How much do you make and what do you do for your money?"

"One night, I was waiting on a bunch of college students and not only did they stiff me on a $60 tab, but they drew a picture of a dick on the check. I cried.

"It reminded me of when I was in college and we would go to this gay bar in Greensburg. I didn't know enough to tip then, but I knew enough not to draw a small penis on the check. I feel bad that I was such an awful customer, but working here has taught me the importance of recognizing the value of your server. I would never stiff anyone now.

"Last September (2017), I also picked up an office job at UPMC for health insurance reasons and I am doing well. It's going nowhere, but is a stepping stone to maybe taking some grant writing classes, moving forward. I also think about welding sometimes—there's good money in welding.

"I talk about this place a lot. People say if you can serve here, you can serve anywhere. It's funny the impressions that people have about the service industry. They ask, 'Do you drink on the job?' We're not idiots. We have fun but we don't drink. Why jeopardize a good gig?

"I like the people here first and foremost. I've made so many friends here. Truthfully, who I am now, this is the person Kellie wanted to be, except maybe with a hot husband. She grins. Maybe I am where I need to be."

Tina—Dance Party

Tina is sharp and blunt at the same time. A tell-it-like-it-is kind of person with a delicate curiosity; she will never forget the day she started at The Cage. Tina trained on Thursday for a mere 4 hours with coworker Amanda. The next night, Friday, was the annual Dirty Limerick contest (one of The Cage's biggest nights besides Halloween), which Amanda was supposed to MC, but didn't show.

"Everyone loved Amanda," says Tina. "She was the kind of waitress that would sit down in your booth and tell you something personal about herself, ask you what you're up to—she was open." That is not Tina's bag. She is far more private, but learned something from Amanda's gregariousness, something about making tips and friends.

So, Tina had never served a table in her life, let alone handwriting checks for every order (yes, we still do the carbon copy check book). She had done design work

in bars, but knew nothing about beer—or dirty limericks. "It was the night from hell, except really funny," says Tina ten years later (her decade anniversary was March 17, 2018), now that she has figured it all out. "Years literally fly in this place."

Tina grew up in Greenfield/Squirrel Hill and went to Allderdice and then CAPA (Pittsburgh's Creative & Performing Arts School) for visual art. She comes from a family of artists. She left home at 18 and went to college at Pratt Institute, eventually doing sculpture work for an interior designer.

Tina moved up fast, grew with the company, was good at what she did and liked it a lot. She worked from home, made her own hours, but still, something didn't feel right—it was not how she saw her life. She still wasn't producing her own work. Though she made good money, she left—a decision she still questions.

"When I moved here, I knew I needed to do something mindless." Tina was going through a breakup after 14+ years. She would return to New York to do freelance jobs every other weekend, but soon tired of that. Today, in addition to her work at The Cage, she sells vintage clothes at pop-up events on the side. It's enough to keep her toe in a creative venue and still allows her to work as one of the most popular servers at The Cage.

"I have almost quit like three times," says Tina. "When our deep fryer broke for five months and four days (yes, exactly that long), it was so hard. People would yell at us and leave without paying. That's not the way I would normally characterize our customers, but when they can't get fries and hot balls... it was a dark time. We all stayed through that, so that says something about how much we like it here.

"I wouldn't say it is 'rewarding,' more like spending time with family. We've been here for so long. I actually cried when Caitlin left. She's one of our best friends. Caitlin actually met her husband here."

And, Tina met Alex, now a cook at The Cage. "I try not to slip and call Alex 'babe', try to act like he's not my boyfriend," says Tina. "Work is work."

"Customers move away, try to find their 'Cage'. But, no other place in any other city is the same—everything from college students to mill workers, gay, straight and everyone else along the spectrum, all different colors and races. It's like world peace in a dark, smoky, comfortable place"

"If I didn't like it here, I wouldn't be here. It's my home base—I can't seem to stay away. I like coming here on my day off. It's like not going out, because it feels so much like home. Plus, we get a discount on drinks and food—everything we order. So, it's kind of fiscally responsible, too."

A sad day at The Cage

Alex—My Kind of Bar

"I have been coming to The Cage going on seven years now. I have known Matt for 10 years and have been dating Tina for five. I know it's been said, but it feels like home—a first or maybe second home. So, when they asked me to take a couple shifts as cook each week, I automatically said yes. The first day here. I already knew everything.

"I love that The Cage is comfortable and non-assuming, like walking into Cheers. I know 90% of the people here, and those I don't, well, I get to know them. Every day is different, but really, it doesn't change. There is something nice about that. Plus, I get to work with my girlfriend.

"Growing up in Squirrel Hill, it was clear that everyone came here. I met Jan when I was working next door at Uncle Sam's. Now I work at Point Brugge North as a server/bartender on Mondays and Tuesdays.

"My first day working The Cage, Anthony Bourdain came in for a piece he was doing on Pittsburgh. He ordered a burger medium rare. A month or two later, Benicio Del Toro of Steven Soderbergh's "Traffic" fame came in. He ordered two burgers, one with no bun He ate them in like two minutes and signed the menu. FAME!

"Face it. Everyone loves really good pub food at great prices. That's what we have. Plus, there is a sense of pride in what we do. That's why the customers keep coming back."

Alex's background includes cooking with his mom and working at a pizza shop at age 13 to learn the ropes. Then, he bounced around from restaurant to restaurant serving, bartending, managing. His path was to be an electrical engineer like his mom and dad, but he chose a different one.

"I went to school for psychology and believe it or not, I really like the social aspects of cooking. I am comfortable and enjoy it. I make decent money, but mostly I like the study of people when I am here. It's a learning experience every day. This is my kind of bar. There aren't many others like it."

Below (L to R): Billy, Matt, John, Evan & Alex

Above (L to R): Tina, Chris, Kellie, Jan & Carly

Rome Wasn't Built in a Day…

Current Cage Owners Patty & Rod Oliverio

"We are kind of 'hands-off' owners because we trust our staff, who have been here a lot longer than we. We bought The Cage in 2004 because we were friends with David DeLallo and his dad. We knew Ronnie was not well and wanted to sell. Our idea was to stay true to the 'legend' of The Cage, returning it back to its heritage of high booths and dark, but intimate dwellings.

"We wanted the 'old Cage' back so we dismantled the clinical 'McDonald's booths' and tried to return the dining area to its common ground. We put the iconic booths back in, inviting customers to indulge in a kind of connection they couldn't find anywhere else. So, we lost a booth…

"Rod has been in the restaurant industry forever. I didn't know. I had a lot to learn. Fortunately, Jan & Bill worked for

Ronnie and they made the transition easy. Everyone working here now has been with us for a long time. Tom, who recently left, was here 10 years. We believe in creating a workplace that is friendly, open-minded, hospitable and profitable to all of our employees.

All that we've done is improve quality of food, which was not bad to begin with. Clearly, people loved it. And, we have only increased our prices slightly once in 14 years. I think we are still the go-to place for lunch in Squirrel Hill. We don't compromise on food. Like your mom wouldn't make you a grilled cheese with processed cheese food and a hamburger with anything less than fresh-ground chuck. We want people to feel at home.

"We still make homemade soups and dips from scratch. Our fried cheese balls are a destination food, because we buy the best. Rather than frying cartons of pre-packaged fries, we hand-cut fresh potatoes. A bar is a bar, but when the food is good … and we still allow smoking because we fit within the realms of how much food you can sell vs. non-smoking. Our customers like to smoke. So far, we haven't seen any attrition…

"And, our staff is educated. Matt tests every new beer we sell. We rely on his recommendations because he KNOWS beer.

"As far as the way we run things, it is like family. Everyone knows their shift and if they need to switch, they get someone to cover. I don't worry, because we are a team like that. No one wants someone else to be in the lurch. I don't have to make a weekly schedule. Everyone just pulls through for each other. That energy is part of what makes The Squirrel Hill Cafe special. We are like family.

"As far as being a Pittsburgh tradition, an iconic bar, we are. Everyone has been here one time or another and they all have an

experience—a story to tell. I am hoping this book opens the door to how The Cage has served as a meeting place, a comfort zone, a relaxer in so many lives.

"I am proud to be a part of this heritage and intend on making it last."

The Lion & The Lamb

When Patty and Rod took over the bar in August 2004, it was a big change for everyone, especially Jan, who works daylight and was more likely to interact with the new owners. "It was the first time I would have a female boss," recalls Jan. "But I wasn't as worried about that as I was actually scared of Rod."

Rod is a big man with a big presence and a booming voice, intimidating some might say, and Jan was definitely intimidated. "You know when he walks in a room."

"I was actually terrified of Rod," admits Jan. "But, as the years went by, I learned a little bit about him. Ends up, he's funny as hell, a great businessman and he has likes and dislike just like the rest of us. But he can let them be known—very clearly. That's the scary part. And, get this: he can play a mean keyboard and loves Frank Sinatra."

To Jan, change meant trust. She needed to trust the new owners and they, her. "Patty has never lost her temper with me," Jan says. "Although she's had good reason to. Lord knows, I make mistakes. She has never even raised her voice.

"More importantly, she is on top of the business. She makes sure we are serving quality food and keeps up on the latest beers. Her signature pepper rolls, spinach and artichoke dip and sausages are great sellers. Of course, we are known for our fresh-cut fries and don't forget the hot balls! Patty orders all of this stuff so we don't run out. I feel totally comfortable that she is keeping us in a position to stay busy and keep our customers happy."

Past Cage Crew
A.K.A. Revolving Door

Carly—School of Hard Knocks

The sme day I chatted with Kellie, I had a sit-down with Carly. Kellie goes to sit with Jan and they order the famous hot balls. Carly sits down in the booth with me, a pack of cigarettes, a full Red Bull and is so full of certainty, you can almost touch it. She is The Cage Kitchen Manager, with a short shock of brown hair that she covers with a signature bandana when she cooks. She has a quick smile and is immediately engaging. Her energy, a magic of sorts:

"I've been hanging out here since I was 21 and now I'm almost 36, so that's like 15 years. During that time, I became good friends with Tom, who had been Kitchen Manager/Chef here for more than 10 years. He was the best. He recommended me to Patty for the job and I was chomping at the bit to take it. I came in in August of 2017 and Tom left in September. I got a month's personal training before I was on my own.

"It's true, I have no culinary degree, except the school of hard knocks. But, I'm proof that practical experience counts more than training, and I don't have any debt from school, so there's that.

"My experience? I have been a sous chef for Richard DeShantz, Chef and owner of Meat & Potatoes and Butcher and the Rye. I started with an entry-level position and learned a lot from my mentors: James Ciminillo and Nicky Gendel., Nicky, who was a sous chef, taught me classical French methods/technique, and James, just about everything else.

"When Tom approached me in 2017 to take over the kitchen at The Cage, I was ready to take a break/try something new. It was gratifying to know that with me, he he felt hewas leaving the place in good hands.

"Much like Ronnie, I've heard, I am proud of our homemade soups. The Cream of Potato (that's Jan's favorite) and Broccoli Cheese are actually my mom and grandma's recipes adapted for restaurant volume. I make them in the morning as early as 7 a.m. (sound like anyone we know?) I also make my stocks from scratch, grate cheese by hand, so everything has the love in it. I truly feel that when I am in the kitchen, my grandmother's spirit is watching over me.

"For instance, my grandma measured everything with a teacup. You never see that in recipes. I believe that the heart of cooking is watching other people and passing on traditions. It's a sincere form of non-verbal communication. I make almost everything myself, including fresh chili every day. I make it with ground chuck from a small old-fashioned butcher shop. They grind it fresh for us. It's part of my secret recipe (she winks).

"I love that everything I cook is quality—The Cage doesn't skimp on ingredients. When you come in and sit down, you feel that someone is cooking just for you—the taste, the aromas. Even the cheeseburgers are an act of love. We use the same fresh-ground chuck we use for the chili and take care, pay attention to the temperature. If you want it medium-rare, you will get it medium-rare. There is a sacred trust involved in ordering food. I mean, a stranger is preparing it for you. I stand up to that. We have the best bar food—top tier in the city of Pittsburgh—hands down, no question.

"Some things are not homemade, of course, like the cheese balls, but they are the highest quality frozen version you can find, and we serve them with our marinara sauce, so really, they deserve their high ranking on our menu.

As UPS drivers in the general Squirrel Hill area, we make a point to converge on The Cage as often as we can for the great food, great service and of course cheese balls! Thank you for always giving us a great lunch break!

—***Dan Miller & Chad Taylor***

"I know it sounds corny, but we really are a small family. Not one can exist without the other in this grand machine called "The Cage." Three weeks ago on a Saturday morning, we did more than $700 in sales—just Jan and I. We rocked it out for five hours. There is a sense of powerlessness that can overcome a cook: orders just keep coming. It's a moment of ego; I determine everything—some weird psychological thing. I know it's there, but it's not me. I just go with the flow.

"And, I love working with Jan. We get along like bread and butter. We have these great moments, like singing Christmas carols in the kitchen. Where else do you get that? I stopped drinking about four months after I started here. Jan doesn't drink either. There's no pressure. Everyone respects everyone else.

"So, yes, I am happy here. I like the neighborhood and being a part of a grand old Pittsburgh tradition, but I also have a vision. I would like to bring back some more time-consuming foods, like pierogis. It's a project of passion, but I think I can make it happen.

"Professionally, I'd like to bring the cuisine into the 21st century without dismissing tradition. I don't want to disservice history or our customers. Frankly, I'd like to have more homemade veggie options.

"Not all of my decisions sit well with everyone. We have this book behind the bar called the "Rant Book" and we're all free to write in it. Patty reviews it and addresses any conflicts. One of the waitresses didn't like my coleslaw. I make two: one with mayonnaise, mustard, vinegar and slaw, and a simple vinegar slaw with jalapeño. You can have either or both. That's my new thing. I think I won that rant.

"Mostly, I just want everyone to feel welcome and get a great meal (at least before midnight). When I worked as a server at Aladdin's for a while, we would all come down after work, and we still have reunions here. I have great memories; it is such a good bar for that."

As we finish, I thank Carly for her candidness and enthusiasm. The night feels like a lovely balance of insight and information. I grab a cheese ball on the way to the bathroom. When I come back, Jan, Kellie and Carly are packing up to go home. I ask Matt for our bill and he says, it's already been paid and hands me the leftover cheese balls to take home. Like I didn't see that coming …

Kira—Staying in the Game

Kira is a woman of the world. She grew up in Minnesota, New Mexico and Seattle and studied abroad in Belgium her senior year of high school. She did her undergrad work in theater at Macalester College in St. Paul Minnesota and then came to Pittsburgh to get her M.A. in Creative Writing (creative nonfiction) from Chatham on the urging of her professors and mom.

But Kira didn't necessarily want to be a writer. She wanted to be an actress. She graduated from Chatham four years ago (2014), which is around when she started working at The Cage, which is what all good liberal arts graduates do.

She sits down with a POM juice and a cold (no one calls off with a cold at The Cage). Bright, articulate and ready to talk, she tells her Cage story with something slightly less than enthusiasm, but with a warmth that is reaching.

"I worked at Dunning's Grill in Regent Square, a mile or so away, for years when I was in grad school. When I found out it was closing, I got a job here. I started on the same day as Kellie."

Her description of The Cage begins: "The characters that reside in this odd, unique space that hasn't changed in 30 years are charming and maddening. You can't find this zeitgeist anywhere else. It is a small staff and everyone is completely character. Like Jan carding 40-year-olds and Billy with his giant beard and biker clothes. Plus, it's really cheap.

"Of, course I like it here. Where else would you find an experience like this? Meeting people you would never meet—everyone has a story. I've spent the last four years trying to get to know everyone, trying to recreate my experience at Dunning's, which was like family. This is just a different family. Dunning's was overpriced and the food wasn't great, but everyone knew each other and had your back. The Cage feels like that to me now—though very different."

This is when a man approaches our booth and asks to buy a cigarette from me. I hand him one and say "no worries," but he leaves a buck on the table explaining it pays for his guilt. Kira says, "he's already hammered."

"Working here is insane. I thought I was a solid server before I came here. Then, I got my ass served to me. It looks little: 10 booths and 4 tables. How hard could it be? Learning to work here was a long and difficult process, but I think

I've got it now. People can't hear my name (it's so loud) or call me Carol, so now I just go by my nickname 'Kiki.' It's easy for them. I like to make things easy.

"Wednesdays and Sundays I am here by myself with just Billy behind the bar and we get slammed. But you just have to do it—get through it. Find a way to stay in the game. There's a lot more young people here, unlike Dunning's. There, a table might order a round or two; here, they just keep coming. Everyone wants more and more. I try not to panic. I learned the hard way.

"Honestly, I love security and comfort of having a steady job. I work three nights a week and then in the warmer weather, I also work at Redfin Blues on Washington's Landing. That makes summer a little more busy.

"I rarely have a bad night here because I know how to be here. It's comfortable and the money is good. You always make something."

(L to R): Kellie, Chrisy, Kira & Tina

Evan—A Cage Story in the Making

Evan is possibly the cutest chef in town. I say this because when he leans over the counter to take a sip of coffee and a drag from his cigarette, then smiles, the word "cute" comes out of three people's mouths. It's a burden to bear.

One of the newest Cage members, he began work in September of 2017, recruited by Carly, whom he knew from their time together at Pittsburgh's Pork & Beans. Today, he works 4 nights a week, 4 pm to midnight or 1 a.m., depending on the crowd.

"Carly's my boss, but I work alone—no one barking orders at me; I like that. I like being my own boss and Carly trusts me. If I ever have something different I want to try, she just says ok. I think I'm spoiled now; I can't work under anyone again.

I notice a couple of scars on his arm. "Those are burns," he says, shrugging. I'm good, but still a little clumsy.

"I've been working in kitchens since I was 14: washing dishes, chopping onions, working the line. Everything. I've worked in soulless places that are like machines—no personality or creativity. This is the exact opposite. The food is great, I take pride in what I make and people actually appreciate it. Yeah. I'm sure you've heard this before, it's the people.

"And there's a reason they come here—I like to think it's the burgers. When someone asks for a fried egg on top, I'm like 'oh, yeah.' I've always been cooking but I probably wouldn't be if people didn't like it so much. I make a pretty damn good burger.

"When I started—which wasn't long ago, comparatively—I had to figure out people quick. I think I learned 100 names in the first week. I know people were like, 'who the hell is this guy?', but to this day, somebody always buys my first drink. I guess I don't really have a Cage story yet, but I am sure it is coming."

Tom Tantlinger— I Love This Place

Tom is as unassuming as you can imagine. In a nondescript t-shirt/jeans/baseball cap, sipping a 16-ounce Budweiser, he sits down in the booth with a smile and a very "what is it you want to know" attitude. The Kitchen Manger at The Cage since 2007, he has seen a lot and still comes away saying "I love this place."

"I used to work as a prep cook at Aladdin's and would stop in to visit Jan. One day, Jan says they need a cook. I was just clowning around. Never figured I'd get a job. But, Patty hired me on the spot. I remember eating a big ham sandwich and feeling perfectly at home, excited to have some more control over the menu.

"I didn't go to school, but I am a chef by trade. I've been in the restaurant industry since I was 13. I've worked all over the place: Cleveland, Jeanette, Greensburg, Pittsburgh—they're all my kickin' areas. I ran Piccolo Piccolo downtown for 3-4 years. It was a number one restaurant.

"My goal when I came here was to make the menu more 'homey' with more homemade stuff—soups, specials, Patty's ham sandwich, meatloaf and mashed potatoes; corned beef and cabbage on Saint Patrick's Day …

"Every day I'd show up two hours ahead. I was in full charge of buying ingredients for the soups, sauce, chilis (my buddy Jimmy (of Jimmy and Tracey) loves my chili). I do what I got to do, take pride in what I do.

I will always remember Tom the cook. He always had a story and couldn't wait to get done with his shift, come around to the other side of the bar, and tell you all about it.

One night, I sat with him way too late, and outside a blizzard had covered Squirrel Hill with ten inches of snow. My car and my apartment were each about the same distance away, but in opposite directions. Wanting to make the next morning easier, I chose to go to my car and drive it home.

The car was buried and after an hour I decided to just spend the night in the car. Imagine my surprise when my wife and Tom woke me up at 3am.

He had helped my irate wife find me after she went to The Cage to find my silly ass when I didn't come home. I'm not sure if I should be grateful or pissed. I'm still digging myself out of that one.—Tom Murton

"Me and Jan had a great time. One time, she was in kitchen and stuck lemons in her bra. She walked around for like half an hour and nobody even noticed …

"Four years ago I lost my son. The Cage gave me so much support through all that. When I came back to work, the other cooks encouraged me to stay home and give myself some time. I wouldn't. I am dedicated to my job; have always been like that. I like to work and being here every day made dealing with a rough couple of years easier.

I hate to say it, but I spent almost every day here drinking until 2 a.m. and coming back in the morning. This bar never changes. The loyalty of our regulars is incredible. I've met a lot of really, really good people. Once they get to know you, it gets to be a lot of fun. Did I say I love this place?"

(The best part is the apostrophe)

Caitlin Avon—Growing Up in The Cage

"I met my husband here," begins Caitlin. I kind of feel like there is nothing more to be said. "Chrisy, Tina and Matt are my best friends. Like family, and Billy…"

But there is more to be said. Having worked at The Cage for seven years, Caitlin still holds a strong place in the Cage zeitgeist. She grew up in Penn Hills and was working at a bank when she saw the infamous "Waitress For Hire" sign on the The Cage Door. She had waitressed since the age of 16.

"Tina started two weeks before me, " she recalls. "So, we kind of embarked on the journey together. Eventually, I quit the bank and worked at The Cage full time. I worked nights. I worked with Jan in the days and I bartended for Jan on and off.

"What I discovered here is that as long as you are yourself, everybody is welcoming. There is a real warmth in this space. I grew up here; it made me who I am, helped me discover who I want to be and what is important. It is a support system that most would not recognize. I traveled through my formative years with that support and trust. It is part of who I am."

Caitlin's husband worked up street at The Exchange. He came in often and she had a crush of him, but was afraid to talk. One day they did and then they moved in together. Yet more evidence that The Cage is a hotbed of romance and connection.

"Yeah," she says. I still come here pretty often, but I don't feel like it's nostalgic as much as I feel like it's home."

Les—1980-Something to 1990-Something

Ten Years in 'The Cage'

Mostly I am good
with Jack, offering to get
him coffee or a Coke,
to call a taxi or a friend.
But nights when the gin
takes a back seat in his mouth
and he waves his glass,
spitting "pussycat" in that tired
late-shift slur, I turn and wait
for him to leave; the tide
of regret rising like the sharp
corner of a table — his belch
as he stumbles on the way out.

And it's thick some days,
the way you only hear
the baseline on the jukebox,
the air draped with that flat
fryer-smoke smell. Billy
in his sixth year of six nights
a week behind the bar,
6 p.m. to 2 a.m.
The revolving door
of waitresses — all writers
or Deadheads, lesbians
or psych majors — struggling
to pay rent, to get by;
too dull to figure tax
on a 2-dollar hoagie, but
sharp as tin at totaling tips:
they *never* get stiffed twice.

Me, I work both sides
of the bar, stragglers
and sophists knee to knee
on a plowed row of stools,
straddling an Iron and a shot
of Windsor. Friday nights I find
my place in line, drink
for free; bathroom graffiti
like "my karma ran over
your dogma," rescued
from tiled obscurity,
old lovers dropping by
with memories as soft
as their bellies, kisses weary
as the fading neon,
last call rising
like the moon
over Forbes Avenue.

— Leslie Anne McIlroy

Leslie Anne McIlroy, an advertising copywriter, lives in Regent Square. Her poetry placed in the National Poetry Hunt, sponsored by The McGuffin magazine, and has recently appeared in The Eclectic Literary Forum.

15 Years After 'The Cage'

I dreamed I was working at The Cage again,
but the draft was kicked and the regulars
all parodies of themselves (which isn't really
a dream) and there were lots of girl bartenders,
which is totally a dream, and I didn't like it.

I wanted just Billy and me, and room
to get to that thirsty boy at the end.
I wanted to stock the beer, rotating bottles
to keep things fresh. I wanted the dumb
waiter, but then the glasses kept breaking

and that was enough to wake anyone up,
but I was clinging to a spire out back
of the bar, my insulin pump crashing
to the ground far below. That's what
I remember, hanging on, looking down.

That, and Ronnie, the owner, telling me
death wasn't like this. It was more like
opening the bar door at 5 a.m. to make
soup and finding your bartenders drunk
on the bar stools, a bottle of vodka

between them, tips divided, ketchup
bottles full and the cash bag delivered
duly to the bank after close. It was more
like emptying the ashtray, pouring them
a shot and sending them home to sleep.

— Leslie Anne Mcilroy

Leslie Anne Mcilroy (lamcilroy.com) is a writer living in Wilkinsburg. Her collection "Liquid Like This" was published by Word Press in 2008. (Her previous poem about the Squirrel Hill Cafe, "Ten Years in 'The Cage,'" was published in the Post-Gazette in September 1996; it appears with this poem online at post-gazette.com/forum/comm).

I don't remember a lot, but that is true of my entire life. I don't remember how I was hired at The Cage or my first shift. I remember it was back in maybe 1985; I remember thinking it was cool. What wasn't cool was "Import Nights." On Tuesdays and Thursdays we would sell imported beers—Heineken, Coronas, Labatt's,—(long before craft beers made their mark on the scene) for the ridiculous price of $1.15, which meant 10¢ tips were an easy option. I cursed Ronnie for that—and it was busy. With only one waitress to cover the whole bottom floor serving booze and food, it was a cluster-F.

But I liked it. I liked waiting on people. I liked the fryer grease-smoke smell of my clothes after a long shift. I liked filling the ketchup bottles at the end of the night. I liked the possibility that I would meet someone, anyone, THE one. I worked both days and nights as a waitress while figuring out what to do with my last year of studies at Carnegie Mellon University.

I decided to take a semester off and do an internship at Carus Publishing in LaSalle-Peru, Illinois (exciting, right). There I

took a second job at a restaurant where I was hired as a bartender. I lied and said I had bartended in Pittsburgh and spent my days studying the *Mr. Boston Official Bartender's Guide.* The clientele demanded lots of frozen daiquiris, old fashioneds (can you say "muddle"), sidecars, martinis and more. When I got home to Pittsburgh a year later and needed a job, I told Ronnie I had bartended in Illinois. Making gin and tonics, pouring drafts and the occasional snakebite was a cinch.

For years I worked Thursday, Friday and Saturday nights with Billy. We were the ultimate team. We were both absurdly attentive, getting to customers within a minute of seating and fast on our feet. Physical things would upset Billy; emotional things would upset me. We had each other's backs. If a bottle or a glass broke, it would piss Billy off; I would immediately clean it up. If someone was rude or off-color or even slightly obnoxious, Billy would handle them and set them straight or kick them out (usually the latter).

I remember once Billy actually jumped over the bar to break up a fight. He kind of kicked / kicks ass as a bartender.

We learned a lot about each other on those long nights, sharing secrets, observations and trying to figure out what the fuck was happening next.

Once, Billy & I decided to go Christmas shopping together—a thing we both hated. We went to the long-defunct Century Three Mall and about an hour in, gave up and went to The Oyster Bar, as I remember it, but that's probably not right. As I said, my memory does not serve me well. Suffice it to say that our shopping mission was less than a success.

We became best friends. We never drank when we worked. But afterward, when all the barstools were placed neatly on the bar top so the floor could be cleaned, the doors were closed and the lights were dim, Billy and I spent hours pouring drinks and talking until 4 am. We always went to the liquor store the next day to replace the bottle we drank. Not that Ronnie would mind us having one or two after close, but three or four …

What was a success, in some weird way, was my love life at the Squirrel Hill Cafe. To this day, everyone I have loved, I met there—and some, I didn't—didn't love, I mean. Patrick had just come to town to do his MA in Library Science. At the time, I had taken a second job at the Original Hot Dog Shop (another Pittsburgh institution, now permanently closed due to the pandemic) and he came there to see me on one of my first and only nights—the job was awful. That night, I gave him a lift home to Squirrel Hill and it was love—until it wasn't. Patrick ended up bartending at the Cage, too, and left town with a Cage waitress. Another workplace hazard—not worth mentioning.

Danny was a regular who I used to share poems with. He drank vodka on the rocks and would come in early. We spent many nights drinking at The Cage and wandering off to his apartment on Darlington Ave. Though it didn't work out, we remained good friends to his end. Danny left us on May 20, 2018—far too young. I still look when the Red Door opens to see if it is him.

I also met the father of my son there—on my birthday. We hooked up online and decided to meet at The Cage after work. It was love at first sight. He gave me a Buena Vista Social Club CD and we spent the next three days together, and then the next seven years. We still meet at The Cage when we have things to talk about. Even hard things. Everything is better when you are in a place that knows your name (yea, I made that up), your drink, your loves.

Finally, I met my last love, Don, at The Cage. He swears I must have waited on him years before, but I don't remember (see a pattern here). I was meeting him because I sent him a resume and I thought he needed a freelance writer. Four hours later, I got no freelance, but I did get a new lover, who would inform my life in ways no other had and become a seminal part of my adult "growing up." For the years we were together, we spent many hours at The Cage, so clearly in love that other customers would tap us on the shoulder to say so. We met artists and musicians, writers and lawyers, even a seer. And, had many a shot of tequila…

A couple of other memories stick, like the now defunct Squirrel Hill Happening. It was a little festival of storefronts and food trucks, crafts and the like over a long summer weekend where they blocked off Forbes Avenue from Murray to Shady. Parking was a bitch, but what I remember most is the petting zoo. We would get out of the bar at 2 or 3 a.m. with a couple of drinks in us and there would be llamas in the Church yard caddy-corner from the bar. It was the most surreal and delightful thing. I wanted to pet them so bad, but am not a gate jumper. I miss the llamas—and sometimes the late nights.

The other night that was unforgettable was the night I was bartending and happened to notice that four of the men sitting at the bar had been past lovers. FOUR of them, all at once. I remember praying that they didn't talk to each other and subtly arranging seating to keep them separate. Not sure what that says about me, but remember, I worked there 10 years and I am going to assume this was toward the latter part of my stint.

Finally, the employee toilet. It was down in the liquor room in the basement. Just a little white basement john set amid shelves of liquor. I adored peeing there, surrounded by Absolut and Jim Beam. Again, what does this say about me?
Today, I still drag dates to The Cage. It is like a rite of passage. Plus, it's my favorite bar (stating the obvious), and no matter who I am with, I know I am safe. Almost everyone loves it unless they hate cigarette smoke and then they turn yellow: The Cage vetting system at work. I've since quit smoking, but can always bum one in a pinch (thanks, Cole). I can always get what I need at The Cage.

Mike, Nick & Molly

Walter, who revamped The Cage front

Lou, the mailman

Kristin

John McDonald & friends

A Page in the Cage: Interviews & Testimonials

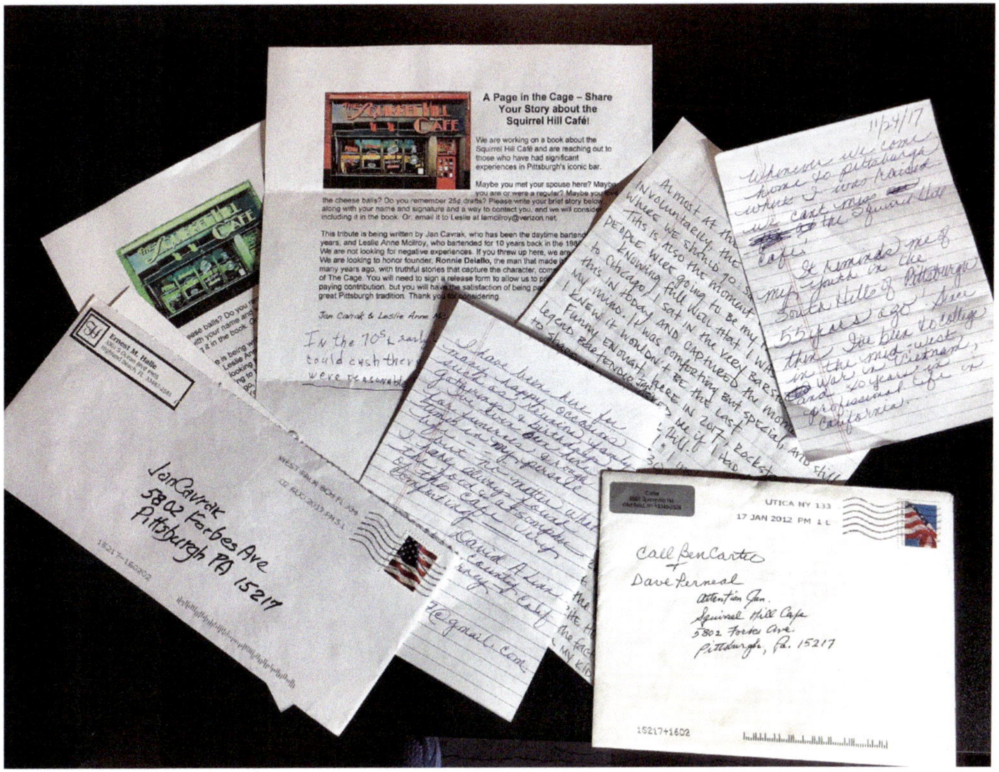

Friday Happy Hour—Our Other Living Room…

… this is Rohit's take on what their regular Friday corner by the windows at The Cage means. For 30+ years, this group has been occupying their street-scape turf from 4 pm to an unpredictable hour of the evening, depending on how many world problems need solving. There have been some fluctuations of participants, but a solid core: Denise, Mary Ann, Stuart, Cindy, Bill, Ginger, Rohit, and Ruby. Jon, Amanda and Chip only have a year or two under their belts.

If there is one thing you can count on for Friday Happy Hour, the gang's all here. And Jan saves them seats …

"When I think of The Cage, I think of Ronnie," begins Mary Ann. She is a light-spirited woman, who I think is part fairy or gypsy. She sways to the music like a flower following light, but is also very thoughtful, intent and beautifully irreverent, noting that she loves the music, but can't really hear it because Jan keeps the volume turned down …

"The sign that was here for so long (where did it go) 'It's nice to be important, but it's more important to be nice,' kind of sums up the whole Cage zeitgeist.

Bill Leidy and Ginger Valcheff met here 30 years ago and are now coupled for life. They are an integral part of the Friday evening festivities.

"This is our corner," says Bill. Some call us the after-work crowd, but mostly I think of us as best friends—family. I remember one time I was here, maybe 40 years ago with two buddies. They were from the Army Special Forces who served in Vietnam. They got into an argument about who could rip a phone book in half. It turned into a fisticuffs and they broke a table. Jan kicked us out. They finished their argument outside, then came back in and had a beer. Educated, uneducated, we all get along."

"What I like," adds Ginger, "is Christmas. Ronnie would allow us to bring food in to share with everyone. That's how a lot of us met—coming here and sharing. Aren't too many places like that. We solve world

problems at The Cage: politics, weddings, funerals. It may sound stupid, but it's powerful. We're giving positive messages to each other. Especially the women. All of us, we're born with sparkles in our veins."

"When I think of Ronnie," says Mary Ann, "I think how he was always outside the bar kind of eying me up. I was a little Italian girl and he liked me. He knew it was not going to happen, but he and I had a connection. I can come here by myself, read a book, have a sandwich. I can leave money and my shit on the bar. No worries. It's certainly not the wine that brings me back. I drink good wine at home. But cheap wine will do when I am here with my friends. Amen to The Cage."

Ruby Ann (whose real name remains a mystery) is typing for me because she, like nearly everyone else, types faster and can capture the conversation. "We're all foreigners in our own way," she says. And then, almost simultaneously, both she and Cindy say "we come here to be with friends."

"You can have a conversation with anyone here," chirps in Cindy. "Billy is the best bar keep ever," says Chip. Chipper came from Netherlands and worked in Pittsburgh for six months. He left to go back home but immediately realized he was missing his new family and came back six months later. "it was like an infusion of love," he recalls.

Speaking of love, "I met my wife here," says Rohit, laughing. "Like I said, it's our other living room, but more like a sectional. We could use a recliner."

Suddenly, Jon and Amanda walk in. They are young and lively with compatible smirks and general coupled warmth. "I love The Cage for SO many reasons, says

Jon. "Like, the people, the buttery nipples (these are drinks made with vodka, Irish cream, butterscotch schnapps and coffee liqueur, not slippery naked women) and the diversity of character. You meet neat people here who become your immediate friends—whether you agree with them or not."

It's at least clear to me that most of them agree that The Cage is truly a "home away from home" with people you choose to be your family.

Minette Seate—Like a Magnet

The Squirrel Cafe had always been part of my consciousness before I ever went inside. Maybe it was the red Art Deco lettering and those crazy cut-out squirrels that beckoned to me. I would stare at it when I was too young to go in, swearing to myself that I would walk through that red door some day and find out what was on the other side. And when I was old enough, I spent many an evening either crammed in a booth or sidled up to the bar for a lot of the 80s and early 90s.

It was the place to meet my friends before heading off to a show in Oakland, or a quick drink with a date before strolling around the corner to the movies. Or a loud, long evening with my brother and a million biker friends. Or alone, especially alone. I never felt nervous or wary about sitting alone at the bar in The Cage. It was just comfortable. You could have a smoke and a drink and watch the world go by.

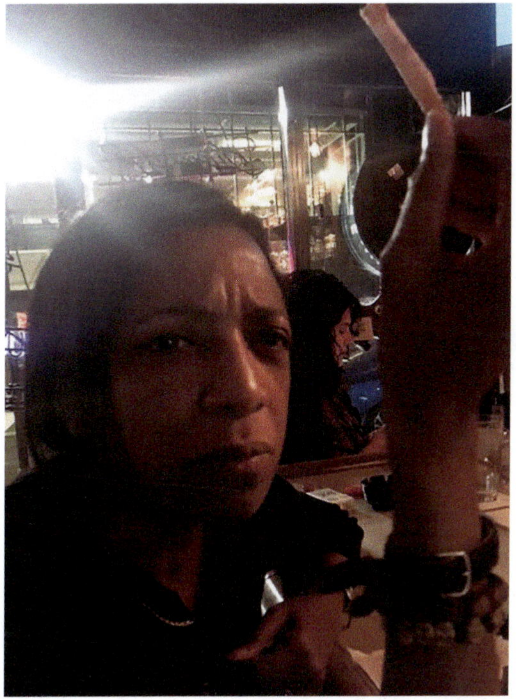

The Cage was like a magnet. We'd go there for a quick one and, before you knew it, two hours had passed and you were waiting for your third song on the jukebox.

It was perfect because my bus dropped me off across from the Rite Aid (that used to be a gas station) on the way in—and stopped right in front of my first single-girl apartment on the way home.

A lot of the people I met at The Cage, I still see today, but unfortunately not nearly as often. Big John and Jan and Leslie and Bill with that Zippo lighter; I swear he kept in a holster.

But it wasn't just the convenience, or the giant fish sandwich or that you could go there with $20 and come home with change. It's because I always felt at home there. I still do. Though I do miss those Benson & Hedges Menthols.

Eric Heyl—Iconic Pittsburgh

Even though the sign says "Squirrel Hill Cafe," the place is simply The Cage, a dive bar in the best sense—smoky, casual, good jukebox and great cheeseburgers.

It's the place where I congregated with neighborhood regulars, blue-collar workers, Pitt and CMU graduate students and the woman I hoped to marry. Given the many nights we spent there, I think the bar deserves some credit for her eventual decision to accept my proposal.

Bill and Jan were the glue that held things together during those days when Ron DeLallo owned the place. He had a reputation for being cantankerous that was well-earned, but he had genuine affection for the neighborhood. If you walked past the Cage early in the morning, you often saw him sitting in the front, gazing at Forbes Avenue passers-by.

You also often saw Ron posting his societal opinions along with the daily specials in

the front window. I wrote a column for the late *Pittsburgh Tribune-Review* once on Ron complaining mightily via the window about having difficulty finding a cook because all of the applicants wanted to be paid under the table.

"You can't just sit around and stew when something bugs you," he told me then. "The only things that should be stewing in this place are the tomatoes."

In 2004, married, with children and no longer a nightly visitor to the Cage, I returned to speak to Jan about Ron. He had just bought a house in Arizona and was planning to move there to open a sandwich shop when he was diagnosed with pancreatic cancer.

Jan didn't want to think of him lying in a hospital bed dying. "When I look around and see that he's not here, I tell myself he's just in Arizona for a while," she said. "In my mind, he's in Arizona."

The Cage is grit and haze and beer. But it is also a collection of personalities, staff and patrons, who have, over the years, made the whole considerably better than what the sum of its parts should be.

When the late Anthony Bourdain came to Pittsburgh in 2017 to film an episode of *Parts Unknown*, he stopped in with author Stewart O'Nan.

Why The Cage? He wanted to see an example of "iconic Pittsburgh." He couldn't have described the place any better.

Ernie Hawkins—We Got It Right

A native of Point Breeze, Ernie Hawkins is a Pittsburgh blues legend and an international blues guitar aficionado. Having studied with blues genius Reverend Gary Davis in New York City at the young age of 18, he learned the lost art of the Piedmont blues, the Delta blues, ragtime and gospel first-hand, and has continued playing to audiences across the world for the last 55 years.

Of course he wound up in The Squirrel Cage. We all do.

"I used to come here to meet Benny, who played bass with me in the Pittsburgh rockabilly band, The 8-Balls. That's how I met Jan. We'd come here, Benny all costumed up with his makeup and earrings. We'd drink, talk and play pinball. That was in the eighties. That's also how I met Bill, Jan's partner, who became a long-time friend, coming to see us at venues all over the city.

"I would also meet local arts columnist, Rege Behe, on a regular basis, who then worked for *The Tribune Review*. He gave us good press and was a true lover of music and words.

"I got my B.A. from the University of Pittsburgh in philosophy and then my Ph.D. in phenomenological psychology from the University of Dallas, but then got swept back up into music, the way the blues do."

"I moved to Texas (1973-78) for my Ph.D., and while there, met a great guitar player named Art Eskridge who grew up playing blues in Texas and Oklahoma. He learned from a great blues man, Poor Bill Miller, in Oklahoma City in the 1950's. After my Ph.D., I returned to Pittsburgh to play with Gary Belloma and the Blue Bombers for eight years. The band was tight. We got it right. There were some challenges (our bass player was eventually killed in Nashville), but that just added to our legit."

Ernie's blue eyes are warm and his memories swelling like an old song he knows by heart. He has the logic of a philosopher, the insight of a psychologist and the heart of a blues player deep in the cerulean of it all.

Eventually, Ernie ended up playing acoustic and traveling with his wife, Nancy, around the world for nearly 20 years with gigs in France, Italy, Spain and Japan (they officially started dating when she showed up at a gig at Gene's on route 51 in a sexy black dress). "Those were the best days of my life," recalls Ernie, touching the brim of his Steelers baseball cap and looking humbly at his hands, wishing guitar on the table.

"She loved to travel. My reputation as a blues instructor got me all kinds of gigs. I was in global catalogs—a lot of exposure as an expert. We spent nearly two decades seeing the world while I was playing." It was a love story that crossed borders. He was/is the shit.

Nancy, his wife, died after a valiant fight with cancer and Ernie continues to honor her support by teaching others the lost art of the blues.

He doesn't come to The Cage too often anymore, now living in an elevated home on the Allegheny in Harmarville with his Jack Russell Terrier, Bozo. But clearly, when he agreed to meet and talk, there was a note, a tune, maybe even a song he recalled as he opened The Red Door.

"The Squirrel Cage is the soul of Pittsburgh. It hasn't changed. The blues are the blues."

Gary Belloma and the Blues Bombers
Compliments of Pittsburgh Music History

The stars of Gene's were Gary Belloma and the Blue Bombers, who were the regular Saturday night house band at Gene's Blues Bar for ten years. The Blue Bombers formed in 1986 with lead singer Gary Belloma, sax player Chris Patrini, drummer Terry Bates, **guitarist Ernie Hawkins,** keyboardist Fred Delu, and bassist Harry McCorkle. The band was noted for Gary's soulful voice and wild dancing along with Chris Patarini playing sax on top of the bar and tables.

During their residency at Gene's the Blues Bombers released two recordings: the "Bombs Away" cassette in 1992 and "Altitude Adjustment" CD in 1995. After the closing of Gene's in 1997, the Blues Bomber moved to three-year stay at the by Buffalo Blues in Shadyside doing Saturday night gigs. They released the "Pack Your 'Chute" CD in 2001 and the "Departures" CD in 2006

Tony Norman—Immersed

After arriving in Pittsburgh in the fall of '87 for marriage to a graduate student and chronic underemployment for a year, it was inevitable that a determinism dictated by a lazy artistic romanticism would force me to find a literary watering hole where I could commiserate with other posers in style.

My colleagues at the telemarketing firm swore by two places: Chief's, a cramped and crowded matchbox of a place in Oakland, and The Squirrel Hill Cafe, better known as The Cage in Squirrel Hill. Both places were thick with clouds of cigarette smoke in those days, a logistical reality that necessitated stepping outside for fresh air more times than anyone would ever have considered cool.

What I remember most about The Cage was being immersed in sound, the noise rendering any conversation a futile series of pantomiming which didn't seem to bother many folks. I would nod my head in agreement, figuring that by faking it, I would still be right 50% of the time Apparently, no one went to The Cage to talk, except me.

When my wife and I moved to Squirrel Hill in 1989, The Cage became the place I would dart into for a quick conversation with my buddy, the poet and bookseller Franklin Lackner, who was more often than not in desperate need of a drink and a smoke.

If I recall correctly, Franklin, who died in the early '90s, had a love/hate relationship with the establishment, but it didn't lead to him being briefly banned there like he was at Chief's. (Or, maybe I have the story backwards.) Because I wasn't much of a drinker, I settled for a relentlessly boring orange juice on the rocks practically every time. And, The Cage's version of bar food was actually pretty good.

I enjoyed The Cage during the day when grabbing a booth was easier than 'The Hunger Games' that prevailed in the evenings; the bar's off hours when none of the hipsters, poets or madmen/madwomen were around. It was at its best when the music was played at a reasonable volume and the smoking was a wisp rather than a cloud. In other words, I preferred the Cage when it was the opposite of its reputation. Still, it was easy to see why it had become so beloved to the town's literati.

We no longer live in Squirrel Hill, but The Cage will always be a part of my history. As time moves on, my memories of that dark bar will become more romantic. When I'm sufficiently old and far removed, I will swear I was only ever there in the evenings belting out ballads, screaming profundities and inhaling the carcinogens of life with all the gusto I could muster.

Chris Natalia—Pinball & Philosophy

Chris is a favorite of Jan's. She asked specifically to have me talk to him and now I understand why. Smart, perceptive, attractive, young and warm, he is one of the many customers who come here to see Jan on a weekly basis.

"I grew up in the North Hills and went to Carnegie Mellon University for Philosophy in the 1990s. I've been coming here since I was 21 and I just turned 43. That tells you something. Today I do product design for InventionLand in RIDC Park. Philosophy can take you so many places and a lot of those places I found talking to the other customers here at The Cage. We had fantastic conversations from cultural theory to linguistic criticism. I was always entertained if not enthralled.

"Jan is a big part of that trajectory. I would come here when I was in school to study and drink. I guess I got kind of skinny. One time, Jan stopped by my table with a burger and said 'Someone ordered this by accident.' She was trying to feed me. It's mostly about her being wonderful. That's why I'm here.

"I moved around a lot back and forth to Chicago, but always ended back in Pittsburgh and here. I guess it's the feeling of the place, the people. It's always comfortable and welcoming. And, they have pinball machine, which is a rarity. There's only one company left that makes them outside of Chicago. I wouldn't say 'addict,' but I like it.

"I come every Friday after work at 2 p.m. Sometimes I go to Jerry's to buy records and then the bakery to buy bread for the weekend. But, then I come here for a cheeseburger and gin & tonic. The burgers are crazy good.

"I have amazing memories and have made so many friends that I met here and hang out with—lifelong friends. And, I've known the staff over so many years; they never fail to get great people to work here. Did I say Jan is amazing?"

Hop into the Squirrel Hill Cafe A.K.A. "The Cage" and you will have a choice of over 130 beers and witness a small gallery of beer promotional plaques. The cozy atmosphere and the funky selections of music on the jukebox makes it a comfortable place to unwind. Happy hours are lively, with an interesting mix of customers. The menu is varied, tasty and well prepared. Both the waiters and bartenders are friendly and welcoming to all. I'd say do a happy hour on a regular basis and you will be glad you did.

—Margery Andrews, Mara Designs

Kathy Clark—No Pretensions

Kathy is the mom. The mom who brought her kids to The Cage for lunch for years, for their 21st birthdays. Today, she remains a mom—everyone's mom. Matronly, wise and often amused, she has known The Cage for almost as long as Jan.

Kathy moved to Squirrel Hill from Boston in September of 1979 and The Cage was the first place her new work friends brought her to introduce her to Squirrel Hill.

"I was 26, just out of grad school and came to Pittsburgh for my first job as Director of Hunger Education Resource Center. I've been here for 39 years.

"We would come here after work during the week and on the weekends, too. It was our hangout—always comfortable with no pretensions. I came less as I got married and started a family, but back then, you were able to bring kids here and what better place to have lunch?

"I would bring Rene here when Kitty was in kindergarten and it was his favorite. He would order a "Freddie Burger," which he named because Freddie the cook made it just for him. It was a bacon cheeseburger with lettuce, tomato and pickle. Thereafter ever known as the Freddie Burger. Jan used to put Rene's school pictures up behind the bar."

Jan and Kathy are old friends and you can tell in the way they elbow one another with their stories. "I was on a diet and Jan knew it. I came in and ordered fries and Jan said 'No. You're not having fries.' I looked at her like she was crazy. She said, 'Pull out that picture you showed me of the kids.' I did. 'You want to lose weight to stay healthy for your family and it's my job to see that you do.' I didn't get fries.

"Another time I came in on a Tuesday and ordered a beer. Again, no. But this time it was because it was Election Day and no one can serve alcohol until after the polls close. Jan's not messing around.

"The best (especially with my kids) was when Jan would sit down with us to take our order and chat a bit. They love her. She IS The Cage."

As the kids got older, Kathy would bring work to the bar. She would do financial reports for work, her taxes. "It's perfect," she says. "The booths are like your own private cubicle. I would just spread stuff out and get things done.

"Not only have my kids celebrated their birthdays here, but I have, too. On my 55th, one of my friends hired a guy who used to play trumpet on the street to play Happy Birthday for me. Quite the memory.

"Another time, I was here with a couple of younger African American kids—Brandon and Adrian—who I worked with. I went to go to the bathroom and the ladies room was full, so I went in the men's room. As I came out, some guy coming in looked shocked and patted my butt. I was kind of flattered, if taken aback, and told the story to my two younger friends. When the man came out and started walking out, they chased him to the back of the Rite Aid across the street yelling 'Don't touch my mom!' He was very confused. Everyone calls me 'mom.'

Kathy's son, Manny

Jan & Kathy

"My memories of The Cage are so intertwined with my kids. For us, it was a place where we could come together to celebrate being a family. It's not really a bar vibe in the day, but more a neighborhood place to come. I am blessed that they did and still do like to come here with me. Manny, my son, worked here a couple of times, but I'm sure you'll talk to him about that …"

Kathy & Kitty

(Author's note: We never did get to talk to Manny.)

Kitty Correal—A Lifetime in The Cage

Kitty is artsy: long dangling earrings, a Star Wars t-shirt and an avant-garde smile. Infectious. She sits down in the booth with excitement in her eyes. We are talking about the cover of the book, which she is going to paint. As a lifelong Cage customer and artist, we can't think of anyone better!

"My Mom, Kathy Clark, would bring me and my four sisters and brothers for lunch when we were little. We were quite the brood—five of us born in six years—beelining it to the pinball machine and jukebox (back when it was a page-turner) every time we came in. We just pretended to play pinball …

"I know it sounds crazy, and you can't bring kids here anymore, but I think my mom brought us because the burgers were great and it was a way to model responsible drinking. She would have one beer, we would have a great lunch and Jan was always so awesome to us. We loved to come in and see her. I don't remember ever not knowing Jan! I feel sad that other kids don't get to have this experience now. I remember once she pulled me aside and said, "Don't come in here after dark. Bad people come in here after dark." She was always protecting us.

"The Cage became a tradition in our family. Every one of us came in to celebrate our 21st birthdays. Each birthday, the party got bigger. Rene's (Kitty's younger brother) birthday took up the whole second floor.

"Now, I come in every week or two, and I host the costume contest on Halloween (we literally cut down the cobwebs last year with steak knives). My second-oldest brother, Manny, worked here as cook. The whole family would come in and read. I am always at the bar with a book. I'm straight up here just to read. Sometimes I just try and help out and people think I work here. I am totally psyched to be part of the Cage family that way.

"As kids, we felt safe here and it's the same as an adult. I've known all the people who work here for so long. It makes me feel secure. Most single women who come here feel that. If there's ever an issue, Tina's right on it. Everyone is.

"I moved back from Boston five years ago and came right back here. I don't care for the 'new' scene. I would tell the people I went to college with about The Cage and the booths and the duct system, and they would always say 'that sounds so cool—I want to go to that wooden bar.' I love this place. The only thing that scares me is those stairs …. "

Always Open—Traci Holtzman & Jimmy Hahn

This is a love story. Hard and desperate and tragic and sweet—a love story that could only happen at The Cage. I met Traci and Jimmy on a Sunday evening in booth 3, never knowing they were there to share their epic romance. To tell their story is perhaps, the greatest gift of all. Not only because I am jealous and hopeful, but because Traci & Jimmy are living proof that love is ever-present, ever, ever. Both are extremely attractive in both presence and depth—physically and emotionally. Together, they are enchanting in that hard-ass Cage kind of way.

Traci Holtzman and Jimmy Hahn met in Linden School in Squirrel Hill in 6th grade. They were clearly as connected as two 6th-graders could be and decided to go "steady." That is, until Jimmy saw Traci walking with someone else ... young minds, young mistakes. She gave him back the identity bracelet he had made for her that said "Jimmy." They moved on.

Some 40 years later, Traci's friend found Jimmy's sister on Facebook and asked if she would forward Jimmy's number. That was a "no" in Jimmy's book. But, when he heard who it was, he relented.

At the time, Traci was in a difficult marriage and her son was suffering from cancer—lymphoblastic lymphoma. She was taking care of him and struggling to keep her life together.

Jimmy had divorced his first wife and had dedicated his life to his sons, which in his mind, meant no dating of any kind. He was devoted. He was also caring for his father. Traci and Jimmy talked by phone a few times a year for nearly three years—no mention of ever "getting together."

Traci's son, Stewart, died at age 22, at home in her care. She left the house shortly after, taking only what she needed, no clutter, no chaos. Her younger brother supported her; her husband, an attorney, became an alcoholic. They divorced.

Traci had been a buyer for Albert Nipon, had worked for Chanel in Hawaii and on Rodeo Drive for Bally of Switzerland. Then, she went to law school & became DA in Pittsburgh. She has two other children: Samantha, an actress in Ashville, NC who loves Shakespeare and costume design and a son who is a chef in Pittsburgh.

Jimmy has a "hot" (Jan's word, not mine—she tells it like it is) 33-year-old son Mike, who is a world-traveler. His stepbrother (Jimmy married a second time), Alex, is 21. "They still kiss me hello and goodbye every time we see each other," says Jimmy, whose own physical closeness is part of his charm (he even give me a kiss on the cheek hello). "I am very proud of them both. They are not stepbrothers, but brothers in the truest sense of the word."

Mike's mom was a speechwriter for Senator Byrd. She died from Alzheimer's in a house fire. Mike was saved. He had dropped out of college to take care of her and was the only one she trusted. He did everything for her—bathed her, fed her, dressed her. He was the only one that could touch her.

Alex's mother, Jimmy's second wife, died suddenly. "Things were not good," recalls Jimmy. "Three days before she died I wrote her a note that said 'It's not that I don't love you anymore, I just can't wait anymore for you to love me back.'" Today, he is relieved he never sent it, imagining how it might be to leave this earth with that thought in mind...

Because both Traci and Jimmy grew up in Squirrel Hill, they each have fond memories of coming to The Cage as children, Jimmy, since he was 9 years old. He remembers it being packed for breakfast, lunch and dinner, back when it opened for the mill 3rd-shifters at 7 a.m.

Traci's dad used to bring her in for a Coca-Cola and she remembers it being a big deal—special. How many times can you say that in one book?

Back to the love story. Three years ago, after Stewart's death, Traci was walking her dog in Blue Slide Park, part of Pittsburgh's sprawling Frick Park, and called Jimmy on a whim. And, on a similar whim, Jimmy said that he would be there in 10 minutes.

"As soon as I saw him walking up the hill toward me, I knew it was the same boy/man I fell in love with 40 years ago," says Traci. "I hadn't felt that spark in years. I knew. I simply knew. It amazes me on a daily basis, after so much loss, to be given so much."

At this point they are gazing across the booth at each other with love that can't be found at the bottom of a glass, only at the red door, that is always open, always waiting, if you choose to come in.

"I felt guilty being madly in love after I had just lost my son," admits Traci. "And then, he gave me the bracelet back that he had given me so many years ago. I knew our souls were connected in a past life. He kept it all these years."

"Once we saw each other," Jimmy adds, "this is the first place we came. I haven't had a drink in 20 years as a recovered alcoholic, but our first date was here. We moved in shortly after, but knowing we had to meet each other's children first. That could be a deal breaker. But, of course, I adore her children and it goes both ways."

"We think of ourselves as married, Traci says, reaching for Jimmy's hand. Nobody can measure up to Jimmy."

"Likewise, my love," Jimmy responds. "I just had a dream that we were walking down the aisle. It scared the shit out of me. But they say 3rd time is the charm. It will definitely be a Cage wedding."

Tyler, Jen & Murphy—A Collection of Little Moments

They are like the Three Musketeers, making the booth look like a Barcalounger. No Yuengling for this crew. It's Big Hop all the way. A pitcher and three glasses.

"We're all married," begins Murphy, laughing. He's sporting a Pens cap and looking joyful—yes, joyful—to be here with his two best friends, Tyler and Jen, who are actually married. Jen snuggles into the corner, her brown hair spilling around her face, eyebrows raised, ready, as I slide in beside Tyler on the other side. He is young, attractive, with a refreshing clean-cut, yet knowing look.

This happy trio is exactly the kind of younger customer The Cage attracts. They are smart, comfortable in their own skin and blessed with banter—and history.

Tyler and Murphy grew up together in Squirrel Hill. Jen, originally from Central PA, met Tyler when they both working at Aladdin's up the street—Tyler as a cook and Jen as a server. Murphy was best man at the wedding. Today, Jen works as an administrator at the University of Pittsburgh, Tyler is a chef at DiAnoia's Eatery in the Strip and Murphy, a cook at Shady Grove in Shadyside.

18 months ago, Jen and Tyler moved to DC and The Cage was the last place they came with Murphy. When they came home, this was the first place they came. "We didn't realize how much of a home it had become," says Tyler. When we returned, everyone still knew us. The good times were still here.

"Jen and I started dating before I was 21. We came here for my 21st birthday," he continues. Murphy has spent every birthday here since his 21st. "I worked next door at Uncle Sam's and always wanted to come in. My friends would wave at me from inside the windows when I passed. Now, they close off the upstairs for my birthday. I'm super popular," he says with a wry grin.

Jen chimes in, "This is more than a place for exceptional moments—like birthdays. It's an everyday moments place. We actually did our wedding planning here. So, it's collection of little moments that culminate into a good feeling."

Tyler picks up on the theme. "I think of The Cage as an organic meeting/gathering place. You come in here knowing you will see people that you know. Once, I saw someone from kindergarten. We all end up here after work."

"No, we're not in a rut," says Jen. "Every time we go out to try something new, we end up here. It's simply the best bar in Pittsburgh. And, the cheese balls!"

Keith Taylor—A Great Day

Back in the 1990s, I lived in Greenfield and took the 61C on a regular basis. On a whim one day, I stopped in for a drink and met Jan. She was so kind and nice that I was more or less hooked. The Cage became the place I gravitated to. Tom and Carly were both great cooks and I loved the Italian hoagie. Plus, The Cage has a great jukebox!

I drank Captain and Coke. One evening, I had had so many that Jan made sure I wasn't driving. Made sure I was taking the bus. I was. Jan looks out for people like me and that's why I keep coming back. That, and the fact that I thought I would eventually meet someone. That didn't work out, but it doesn't stop me from returning.

I like The Cage because it has a very Pittsburgh vibe. It's a working-class bar with people of all races and backgrounds. Everyone's different, but they come here for the same reason. It never fails to be comforting, friendly and fun.

I used to come at night, but now I live in Carrick, so I just stop in every couple of months to say "hi." I don't drink and drive, so now I am a Coke person, minus the Captain.

I keep coming back because I feel like family here. Back in 2012, I was a shooting victim at Western Psychiatric Institute and Clinic. Jan didn't know that I got shot. I couldn't walk for six months. Finally, friends brought me here and Jan was obviously concerned—she hadn't seen me in so long. Imagine a bartender caring that much…

She always asks about my grandkids and my daughter. She remembers shit. Today's the first day I met her daughter Amy, who is doing the photographs for the book. Jan had told me so much about her, I felt like I knew her. To me, that's a great day!

Kevin—Free Refills

Kevin loves history and architecture. Ends up, so does Jan. She speaks of him as an uncommon friend that has given her books and provided many an opportunity for her to have fun. "He likes things a certain way," says Jan. "I set up his place mat in his favorite booth and get him his coffee the second he comes in. Everything as it should be. But, every once in a while when he goes to the bathroom, I mess everything up. Kind of like wrangling a spider's web. He always fixes it and I know he knows it's me. It's a little private joke we have. Its why I love my regulars."

Kevin has been a regular for years and helped us do some research into the history of The Cage. He was the first person to mention that the bar might be connected to the Paterni family, who were also connected to Tambellini's.

Kevin serves tables at Caberet Theatre in downtown Pittsburgh in the Cultural District. "I like history, he says. "It helps you understand things. There are lessons to be learned. It brings a lot forward.

"I actually love history. I enjoy doing it. I'm kind of stuck on genealogy, but it takes time. I come in like six times a week, so I guess that makes me a regular. I work evenings so I come in for lunch.

"Jan does mess with me. One time she brought me my coffee with milk instead of cream—they were out of cream. It was wrong. But I survived. In my mind, drinking is too expensive and you get free refills on coffee!"

A Page in The Cage—First Hand

NOTE: Testimonials were typed in according to what was legible. We apologize in advance for any errors or misinterpretations, name misspellings, etc. Also, they are printed in random order with an eye toward authenticity. Enjoy!

The Squirrel Cage was one of the first bars I discovered after moving to Pittsburgh in 1987—good luck and location more than being in the know. I have been an "irregular regular" over the 30+ years since then, but no bar has delivered more of my favorite experiences. If asked to designate a place as my official second home, there's no competition, it's The Cage.

That "home" quality makes the Cage unique for me. The highest compliment I give any space is to say it feels like my

grandparents' house during the first 30 years of my life, when their house was the central place for family and friends to drink and be loud and real. From first visit and without fail since, The Cage has felt like my grandparents' house.

I'm not sure I can express how important the Cage has been as a place I've always trusted going to, knowing that the staff, long before I knew any of them by name, would treat me as if I belonged there, and knowing, too, that there was a strong chance that other interesting people would be there solo and I'd end up having a great conversation.

I worked a third shift in the late 80s. My version of "late night unwinding" overlapped normal people's lunch, but The Cage was a place where that felt just fine. One day in 1989 I was in a particularly unsettled mood, and after giving up pretending I'd sleep after my shift, I made my way to The Cage. There were probably multiple people there, but in my memory there is just one guy sitting at the bar, a roofer. The TVs above the bar had coverage of the Tienanmen Square protests, and we were both tuned in. Maybe we didn't have the same political views on everything, but we were equally passionate watching those protests. I remember him urging the protesters on, "That's right, that's right, take the fuckers down," and then we bought each other rounds. We didn't talk directly much—it was just sharing that amazing moment in history and that fundamental distrust of authoritarianism that I've encountered in many other people at The Cage.

Another memory—I lived in Regent Square when one of the great loves of my life told me she was breaking up with me because she was running away to New Jersey with one of the best friends of my life. I really shut down for a few days after that (my first experience of how profoundly physical depression can become). Eventually, I forced myself to go out for a walk, and then I ended up walking from Regent Square to Squirrel Hill. I entered The Cage feeling terribly dissociated. I wish I could say I then had an amazing hookup that eclipsed the heartbreak, but what happened was just a good, long, solo drink fest. I am pretty sure this was the first time Billy introduced himself. I commandeered the juke box, played pinball, and mostly just watched everyone else connecting in ways that brought me back to my own desire to connect. By the time I made the long, staggering walk back to Regent Square, I was in a much stronger, more present emotional place.

Experiences like those would be enough to call The Cage "home," but on top of all that, the most profound love-meeting of my life took place at The Cage. In January 2006, the owner of a branding agency I worked for sent me a resume he'd received from Leslie Anne Mcilroy, and asked me if she might be someone to consider for freelance or hire. The resume alone made that an easy "yes," but other credentials—co-founder of HEArt, published poet—made me want to meet her in person. I lived in Squirrel Hill at the time, so I suggested meeting at The Cage. She wrote back to say she had worked at The Cage for years.

We met on a Monday, and one of the highlights of my life was feeling myself literally "falling" in love, leaning forward on my bar stool, feeling every cell reaching out, as she told me about a creative project she hoped to take on. The life-changing love that began at The Cage found new manifestations in many, many shared experiences there, in good times and bad times. That's a whole 'nother book to write, but it reinforces how I've felt about The Cage since 1987—it's one of a few places where I consistently feel like I get to be fully myself and where, any time I go, there is a higher-than-usual probability that something good and wonderful will happen.

—Don Bertschman

The Siren Call of the Cage

I suppose that, as a graduate student, among my most deep-seated fears must be counted the fear that one day I will realize that I dedicated my life to something useless. What I mean by "useless" (or what I think I mean, rather) is something that—after a program requiring five years of my life and numerous sleepless nights—ultimately proves to have been pointless, to have helped no one. But one thing I do not fear is that my time spent living in Pittsburgh will have been a waste.

For the better part of my first three years in this "City of Bridges" I spent my life running along clear-cut lines: Home to Pitt, Pitt to home. That all

changed a little over two years ago when I decided, either by chance or by fate (the two always seem the same in hindsight) to walk into the Squirrel Hill Cafe. Little did I know that walking through that red door would be like walking into another world. Over the next few days, weeks, months, years, I would come to know The Cage—its lingo, its regulars, its steadfast rotation of cooks, waitresses, and bartenders—to the point where I would become associated with my habitual barstool in the front corner.

It's from this vantage point that I've come to consider the world. Torn as it is, my black pleather stool mirrors the person sitting upon it. I am Guardian of the Chargers, a task I don't take lightly. I've witnessed loves lost and those rekindled, Uber rides ordered and forgotten, and the angst of last cigarettes and lost lighters. I've borne witness as countless little dramas have played themselves out over the bar's counter top.

I'm not neutral. Far from it. Many's the time that I have interjected myself into conversations that have gone sour, trying to give assistance to the idle hand of Providence.

Other times I am sought out because it's a well-known fact that I say things, some of them even wise. An oracle to some, I sit back in my seat and direct the fates of patrons who choose to look for luck or love in a back-lit setting.

But more than this, I converse with others about life, the things that happen in the moments between expectation and reality. I talk about what was, what is, and what could be. All hearts break the same and yet upon each barstool sits someone who wants to believe that theirs is somehow different. The floor here is littered with dreams. But the cigarette smoke is a healing balm and the newly filled glasses always produce new dreams.

And still, if you look to the corner, you might see me not as an oracle, but a siren. The song, of course, will vary depending upon what I've been drinking. But most of the time that goes unnoticed. In the world behind the red door, we are each of us many things.

I used to live my life along very different lines, ones that were more clear-cut. But that's what happens after a few drinks at The Cage. We become sirens…we begin to sing.

—Cole Cridlin

You know you're a regular when you walk into a place and your drink is already waiting for you before you walk in the door! Thanks Jan!

I started going to the Cage sporadically in the early 90s, but it was only three years ago that I became a regular. I met someone at a party who introduced me to other regulars at the bar and I was instantly swept up into the mix. Yesterday, I started the early evening off by

Cage Scene by Elizabeth Edelstein

asking Matt, a bartender, "Are you livin' the dream," and he replied "I haven't even woken up from it yet!"

I go to the bar and order club sodas with limes—I don't even drink, but it's such a welcoming, diverse, and down to earth atmosphere that I keep going back. It IS my extended family that continues to grow larger with more friends.

—Elizabeth Edelstein

Cooler Crimes

So I walked into The Cage and a fight broke out between this guy: Old Man Winter and some dude, Peroni! One guy whipped out his White Claw and then the other dude kicked him in the Hiney! Monkey Blood was everywhere! Billy said get the fuck back to Erie! I mean it was like Le Fin du Monde in here! But it was also a Victory cause Molly broke the Ice! She is the Master of Nugget Nectar if ya know what I mean..., a slasher of sorts, she cut a Red Stripe as large as the Great Lakes, right across the dudes' Two Hearts!!!!!

—Elizabeth Edelstein

The first time I went to The Cage was for a group happy hour and it was the first, and to my recollection, the last time I sat upstairs. I don't remember the second time I went to The Cage or the third or the fourth or the fifth. I remember occasionally thinking it would be a good idea to go there and then Bill would show up at the table with wings because it happened to be a free wing night. You could smoke indoors and the line for the bathroom was never long, so it seemed like a reasonable choice for the occasional outing.

There came a time when, due to personal choices, I had to learn what college football was. It was not for me, so I started going to The Cage when the games were on in the interest of making the most of my time. The first time was fine. The second time was fine. And, it just kept being fine. Fine is an underrated

quality in life; it has a calming consistency that many do not appreciate.

I go to The Cage. I sit at table 7. Jan used to come over with a Yuengling, but these days, it is a Labatt's. If you have the urge to socialize or interact, you can. I chose not to for the most part. You can have a table to yourself while you coupon and catch up on routine tasks, having a beer and smoking a cigarette in the process. Or, lots of beers and cigarettes. Day Cage is, of course, much different from Night Cage. Or, Special Events Cage. Night Cage is packed with people giving their lungs a hug whether they are actually smoking or not, and setting the scene for the future when hearing aids will be required. Special Events Cage is the only time it is appropriate to spontaneously hug a stranger—I have done it twice—once when the Steelers won the Super Bowl and once when the Penguins won the Cup.

The Cage is more than a place or the people who go there... It is a collection of nuances that make a community of people who care without necessary intrusion. You can sit alone all day, party all night or bask in the glow of knowing Pittsburgh sports brings everyone together. The Cage is what you make of it, and if you are lucky, you will get to see what The Cage will make of you.

—Victoria

In 2007, the University of Pittsburgh's very own on-line literary magazine, HotMetalBridge.org got its name at the Squirrel Cage. HMB is now a thriving institution in the English Department of Pitt. Here is what happened.

Pitt originally had a stalled-out version of a lit mag called *Nidus*. It turns out that one of the definitions of Nidus is, "a nest or breeding place;

especially, a place or substance in an animal or plant where bacteria or other organisms lodge and multiply" (Merriam-Webster).

What a horrible name! No wonder it did not last. But, under the guidance of the legendary Chuck Kinder, a new crop of Creative Writing MFA students took it upon themselves to reboot and rename the magazine. Many names were tossed about. Among them, *Flywheel, Three Rivers Literary, Steel City Words,* and of course, *Hot Metal Bridge*. These intrepid MFA students met at the Squirrel Cage to enact their final vote on that the new lit mag would be named. After many libations, gridlock, and literary arguments, exhausted by all of it, the recently anointed editor in chief, Dan McMillan, slammed his Sierra Nevada Pale Ale onto the table and declared, "Hot Metal Bridge it is!"

And, to this day, and thanks to the welcoming atmosphere of The Squirrel Cage. May HotMetalBridge.org continue to inspire and grant budding writers a place to exhibit and hone their craft. Thanks, Squirrel Cage!

—Daniel McMillan

The first time I walked into The Cage was almost 40 years ago. We were new to the neighborhood and I was looking for a place for my five-year-old daughter and me to get a bite of lunch. We walked in and backed right out as the place was dark and smoke filled with only a few people slumped over their bar stools—not appropriate for a five-year-old, I thought!

Many years would pass as I walked past The Cage frequently, never going in. It wasn't 'till a few years later when I was in a choir in the area and someone said "Want to go to The 'Cage' after rehearsal?" Thus began a tradition of us filling the long center tables, getting louder and more boisterous with each draft. That's when I discovered that The Cage actually has delicious "bar food" and great soups and divine onion rings—the best around.

Oh, and that five-year-old daughter later formed a friendship with Billy, the long-time bartender! She became a lawyer and practiced in Manhattan for nine years. I'd keep Billy up on her pursuits when we'd come in—including the many marathons she'd run.

My husband and I still drop in occasionally for the onion rings, a burger and beer and always feel at home in the wooden booths with the hubbub, jukebox, friendly staff and customers.

Sometimes we comment on how it reminds us of one of our college haunts at Indiana University where we met. It's true, "you can't go home again," but The Cage is the closest we've come here to bringing back that warm, comfortable feeling of the "salad days".

Here's to another 40 years of good times at the Squirrel Cage!

—Catherine Bomstein

Dear Jan,

It was a surprise opening the box of memories when you called me last week. Thank you for that. My Squirrel Cage friends have become the source of lasting memories over the years. Some shared impressions of living and teaching in and around CMU and Squirrel Hill. Such subjects as girls, fathering children, timeless friendships, and the effect of the passage of time on all of us were discussed regularly.

Sharing common memories, such as service time, sports and school assignments were constantly reviewed. Then, as with all realistic times, one by one we have gone from The "Cage".

The memory of some people is stronger than others. I miss Ben very much. I live alone in the snow-covered woods up in the Adirondack Mountains in northern New Your State. I shall always remember my old friends of The "Cage."

—Love, Bruce

The Cage. You wanna spend a splendorous afternoon after a Manor flick round the block? A good bevvy and a ticket down the levy. An extremely astute recruit. Jan always has a plan. Quick quips—on top of her game.

—Ruby

I'm from Regent Square and worked at Sweet Basil, which was a small, casual restaurant almost on the corner of Forbes & Shady. This would have been in the early to mid 90s. We always came here after work on Friday nights. I don't really have any memorable stories, only great memories and fondness for The Cage. We live in Mt. Lebanon now, but I wanted to bring my husband here for the best burger in town! So happy that you're still here.

—Anonymous

I wrote this in The Cage in 1982:

The wildness called America lives in my blood, put there by the cowboys and Indians when I was just a kid. Do you remember Hop-Along Cassidy, Tonto and the Lone Ranger, Pancho and the Cisco Kid? Well, you can still see them down at the local bar having a few shots for their heads and wondering where all the bad guys went. Hell, they're all unemployed now with nothing to do except tangle with the Sheriff, Jack Daniels, and the boys from the Circle Bar: Jose Cuervo, Yukon Jack Johnnie Walker and his brother; they're a mean bunch of hombres, real Wild Turkeys. Watch out! Watch out! They'll shoot you dead!

I first started going in The Squirrel Hill Cafe in 1978. It was the winter my mother died and I had to fly home from Arizona. It was a time of fate for me because now I'd have to live with and take care of my father, and me and him have never seen eye to eye. What I needed was a focus, something new and different so I started going up to The Cage even though I knew only one person who came into the bar.

It's always easier to go to bars where you know people because one doesn't feel so awkward and all alone, but life is full of challenges and I made one to myself saying that I was going to meet all the local and interesting people who hung out there.

To overcome my natural shyness, I did auto-suggestions to myself thinking four or five times to myself, "I can meet and talk to anyone in the bar." These suggestions actually worked like a charm, for almost immediately after doing it one night, I turned and blurted out something to the guy next to me and soon we were in a lively conversation. I could tell by sitting next to him he suffered from the same bar shyness I did.

I started talking to different people throughout the next three months and soon I made a handful of new friends. Instead of being a stranger in a strange bar staring intently at the liquor bottles, I was relaxed among friends enjoying myself at my own neighborhood local establishment. During my time drinking at The Cage I started a painting business and eventually over the years I hired and taught eight to ten men from the bar how to paint. Guess where we spent the proceeds from our hard work? Of course, at The Cage!

So you see, a little bit of courage and a little bit of mind over matter goes a long way to making life happen down at the local bar.

—Paul Meyers

I first stopped into The Cage because of its neighborhood reputation. It was apparent immediately that it was unique among neighborhood bars. I made new friends here and strengthened old friendships.

There aren't many places around that can provide the different experiences that The Cage does. A quiet lunch, a loud night at the bar with the regulars, and even on busy nights, the booths provide a friends to read or write. The food, drinks and the staff are outstanding. As long as The Cage is around, I'll be coming by for cheese balls and taco nights!

—David A. Bradley

I first went to The Cage in 1985, when I was a graduate student at Carnegie Mellon. Sixty miles away, I was married and raising a family, but to avoid the daily commute, I spent Monday and Wednesday nights in Pittsburgh. I ate most of my dinners at The Cage when I was in town. I sometimes worked on my dissertation there, and occasionally got shit-faced drunk there. I eventually moved to Pittsburgh and still go to The Cage.

I made close friends at The Cage, my circle expanding from graduate students to locals who grew up in the neighborhood. The Cage means affordable beer and good food, but more importantly it means friendship, laughter, sharing, release.

I remember when the big wooden booths and black tables were removed and replaced with smaller, lighter furnishings, presumably to accommodate more seating. When my friends and I first saw it, we said, " It looks like a fucking Burger King!" But we kept coming.

I remember when the wall behind the bar was remodeled with unimpressive pillars and shelving. We said, "What the fuck?" But we kept coming.

I remember when the city of Pittsburgh outlawed smoking in public places, but The Cage was somehow exempt. We said, "Hurrah!" and kept coming to The Cage.

We come for the camaraderie and other constants. We come because the bartenders know our stories and we know theirs. We come because the prices are still affordable and smoking is still allowed. We come because The Cage has the best jukebox, and because the bartenders let us dance when we're so moved, though there is no dance floor. We come because we feel safe there, among friends. We come because our Cage cohort is family. We don't always agree politically or philosophically, and our disagreements can be loud. But we are family.

Now, about those interlopers, who don't know that the corner of the bar belongs to our family at Friday night happy hour: What the fuck?! We-of-the-corner-of-the-bar perform an impromptu serial comedy on Fridays. We do not all appear in each episode, but we need our space. Do not take our ensemble corner seats on Friday. We've had a longer run than the Ed Sullivan Show or, for you youngsters, longer than The Simpsons. Do not fuck with us. We are family.

And to those newcomers, who weren't born when we started coming to The Cage, please do not play selections Friday happy hour that we won't recognize as music. If it will make us want to bang our heads, skip it. If it will make us want to sing along or move our hips/hearts, play it. It you're lucky and persistent, you might become family.

—Denise Troll Covey

A big hello to everybody at The Squirrel Cage. I'm the Little General, a name that Freddy gave me. In return, he was E.T. I worked at The Cage in the middle 80s alongside my brother Ronnie, Freddy, Jan and Tammy. I worked there because one day, when I was unemployed, my dad said, "you can't just sit around the house all day, get to The Cage and help your brother Ronnie." It was a good experience in the world of small business.

Family businesses require a certain kind of skill. I don't know if I had that skill, but Ronnie quickly showed me the ropes and I learned to enjoy it. As the cook, I had a blast. Ronnie taught me how to prep, cook, and how to work with Jan and Tammy. He let me go solo and off I went.

I spoke to Jan lately, and she told me that Ronnie made the best Wedding Soup. Uh huh? I got the secret recipe from Ronnie and then I made the best soup. Making soup was the most fun. Our patrons had to have their soup before they ate anything else. Oh yeah, don't forget the chili. I remember the regulars. The bar was where all the popular people hung out. They ate what I put in front of them with no complaints.

My dad had me introduce desserts to the menu. He gave me $10 a week to buy supplies and I would bake cakes and pies. Can you imagine $10 a week? It sure was a long time ago when you could stretch $10 into a week's worth of desserts!

The most fun was the little kitchen where many of us would work all at the same time. I would fry burgers, toss fries and fish into the fryer, and behind me would be Jan or Tammy, broiling hoagies within five inches of each other, Lots of food flew out of the little kitchen and I think we wouldn't have wanted it to be any other way. It's been a long time since I left The Cage, but I often wonder how things might have changed. I worked at a bar where I was the cook—who else could be that happy?

—Theresa Karl

Stopped in before our show, we're a band from Detroit called Handgrenades. Jan served us well! Great place for a drink and a sandwich. Reminds us of our local watering hole in Detroit.

—Joby Kaslowski,
Andrew Pawelski,
Nicolas Chevillet,
Jesse Shepherd-Bates,
Handgrenades, Detroit

I've been to a lot of bars, and met many people through the years. Every one of them has had their quirks and vibes, but it's safe to say The Cage has been my favorite both for the bar and the people. While I worked down the street for a little over a year, the place was our favorite spot for lunch and happy hour. However, what really makes The Cage special to me are the friends I made there. The bartenders are all great people, and it's safe to say that Jan, the daytime shift, is a good friend. When it came time to make a life change, her advice and our conversations proved invaluable, and for that I am forever grateful. They say bartenders are the peoples' therapists, eh?

—Demetrius A. Nassy

Circa 1999, I would frequent "The Squirrel Cage" to watch Steeler games. I attended Chatham and didn't have a car so could easily walk here, have a few drinks and chow down on a pepperoni roll! Those were amazing and made the stumble back less painful. Thanks for providing a party place to enjoy good football, better food, and the best local Pittsburgh atmosphere! Squirrel Cage forever!

—Stephanie Swift

I never thought I'd be a regular at a bar, yet here I sit some three years in. The Cage is akin to the bar from Cheers. Everybody knows your name. I's a beautiful, dive-y little second home. I am so blessed to know so many amazing people from here. To try and repay all the love & kindness I've been shown, I make cookies to bring in and share. A much beloved recipe is written below.

Chip's Brown Sugar Cookies

1 cup butter
1 cup packed brown sugar
1 cup granulated sugar
3 eggs
4½ cups flour
2 tsp. baking soda
2 tsp. cream of tartar
½ tsp. salt

Preheat oven to 375°F.

Cream butter and sugars until light and fluffy. Add eggs one at a time. Sift remaining dry ingredients. Gradually stir flour mix into butter.

Line cookie sheets with parchment paper. Roll dough into 1¼-inch balls. Place on parchment 2 inches apart. Bake 10 minutes, remove and cool on cookie racks.

—Alex

When does a bar become more than a bar? More than a place to pick up someone or maybe get picked up (not me, of course). A place to wash away your workday woes. When does a bar become more than a place where alcoholics go to fine-tune their addiction.

I know a place. When the person behind the bar is more than a pretty face, (or in Jan's case a SEXY, PRETTY FACE). When you know Tom in the kitchen sees you sitting at the bar and asks "Do you want the usual." Before pretty face Jan has even taken an order. I know a place.

When I leave I'll always get a hug from Jan. Sorry Tom, I only like hugging Jan. Nothing personal. When I ask Jan how her daughter and granddaughter are doing she fills me in. Then Jan will ask me how my dad is doing or how I'm feeling. And then I fill her in. When it's not busy, she will sit next to me and discuss current events. Local gossip. When Tom has a minute, he does the same. Where I can openly flirt with Jan and am guaranteed to get a smile. "I know a place" The street name: It's called The Cage. But everyone else calls it the Squirrel Cage.

—Keith Taylor

My name is Edward D. Russell. I was born in Welland, Ontario Canada. In September of 1956 I came to Pittsburgh to attend the school of architecture at Carnegie Tech and from that time, having located at 1528 Forbes Street in Squirrel Hill, I have been coming to the Squirrel Hill Cafe for a cool beer and conversation.

At the time, the deli was next door and the bake shop was around the corner so I had everything I needed. I am now 82 years of age and come back to see Jan every time I'm in town, which is usually twice a year for school reunions. Nothing has changed at The Cage, which is important to me. I tell everyone I know about this place. Thanks Jan for all the company.

—Ed & Fran Russell

I don't know if the Squirrel Cage's character is Jan or vice versa. However the experiences here, Jan is part of it and it could never be the same otherwise. We basically start with a movie at the Manor, then come here and we have a great time. There is no Squirrel Cage in Charlotte. To say any more would be saying too much.

—Peter Gibbons

Sitting with my best friend from high school at the only bar (that matters) in our neighborhood and reflecting on our teenage years. I realized that this was the right place to be.

—Malcolm Juring

My friends would stop in after Pitt football games in the early 80's where we met Ron. It speaks volumes that The Squirrel Cage is still standing among all the corporate businesses.

—James Ofcansky

I started coming to The Cage at a particularly hard time in my life. Within some time, I became a regular. Shortly after, I started working up the street and would come by before or after work. While I wasn't feeling my best, I had come to make many friends at the bar, and would always enjoy my time there. One particular day, I happened to meet my now best friend Pat. I didn't know it at the time, but the people I met through him are some of the best and most important people in my life.

I hope that I would have met them anyway (seeing as we have many similar interests) but I know that The Cage played an instrumental role in the foundation of many positive relationships that I maintain to this day. I'm so thankful to everyone who made it possible, and I love them very much.

—Evan Khan

I think The Cage is aptly described as "quaint" or "retro." It has a dark, smoky, "lived-in" look (inside and out) which recalls student hangouts in college towns. It does have a huge college clientele, but, as a day progresses, different crowds show up: the lady nurses getting off work, the professors, the techies, the construction workers, the retirees—ultimately an interesting social mix. The possibilities for good conversation become huge. My favorite memories of The Cage include those nights (and days) when I met someone whose personality and words delighted me.

—Ronald Hutson

A shot and a beer are so very near! Now there was a workday mantra that was not only easy to remember, but also, highly inspirational. Our newspaper offices (*The Pittsburgh New Sun*, circa 1977) were above the Squirrel Hill Newsstand, and beside that beloved establishment resided our subsidiary office—our true refuge—The Squirrel Hill Cafe (a.k.a. The Cage). Like any animal refuge, one was likely to hear many strange reports and witness an abundance of novel behavior. In other words, we journalists were perfectly at home and probably spent more hours in that time-suspended tavern than we did at our own homes. This home-sweet-home sentimentality was heightened by the care showered upon us by the daylight waitresses. As I remember it, these elderly women, for the most part, were gently rotund with smiles to subdue the hardest customers. Gravied chicken livers over rice, sardine sandwiches on thick slices of Italian bread and other very affordable tasties were lovingly served at our booth day after day. The standard beverage? A mug of beer. That included breakfast.

I am 110% sure that the story I am about to relate is not unique to myself as a Cage frequenter. The particulars may be somewhat individual, but not the outcome. It was a crowded weekend evening, our booth equally packed with pitchers at various stages of fullness when I spotted a girl getting some change from the barkeep. Pocketing her quarters, she headed for the door, oblivious to the shoulder-to-shoulder patrons who slowed her exit. I jumped to my feet and yelled "stop that girl!" Of course, no one knew which girl in the mélange I was talking about so it became necessary for me to do it myself. Despite the flamboyant theatrics, I must have been mildly charming, because by the time she departed for the Laundromat, I had her phone number. Yes, it really was her number. Our meetings became steady and some years later, we married. That was a night you don't forget.

I'll conclude this "Cage-y" remembrance with a daytime holiday story. It was Labor Day, but the crucial newspaper staff (we put together the pages for printing) was obligated to work.

The day was moving along smoothly amid the continuous sounds emanating from our lifeblood, WYEP FM: Bling Lemon Jefferson, Leadbelly, Bonnie Raitt, Holly Near, Cris Williamson. We were happily going about our business when the editor entered the room and abruptly yanked the radio from its sacred place of honor. Out he went, radio in hand. Jaws dropped in stunned succession. All of us being veterans of the anti-everything establishment movement knew this required a quick response. No word was uttered. We immediately made our way out the front door, down the long stairway, and without hesitation, entered the revolutionaries' stronghold, The Cage.

After several hours of consumption with no signs of negotiation, we assumed we were now unemployed. Bolstered by beer and pretzels, we congratulated one another on our heroic stand. As we were about to corral more beer, our fearless editor sheepishly entered the bar, radio in hand, and set it on the table. "Let's go back to work," he said. When the waitress sat down the fresh pitchers, we looked up at the boss and grinning, he said, "I'll pay for those."

Over the numerous years of daily visitations at the iconic Squirrel Hill Cafe, we believed ourselves to be fixtures in the history of the place that had been home to many a tall, but often true tale, and many a genuine character. For this, I thank you all.

—David Goldstein

In the late 1960's I would take my son, in stroller, to the SHC where I would have a draft "IC". As soon as I sat my son on the adjoining stool, the bartender would produce a small glass of ginger ale and a bag of chips—all without any words or signals. My little guy knew he was in for a treat when we approached the red and black front.

—Michael Chirigos

Having lived in Squirrel Hill many years ago we always make a point of coming back to The Squirrel Hill Cafe for a beer and some local color. We love this place.

—Tony Dixon

In the 1970's, when I worked on the Pittsburgh New Sun as events editor, we used to come here after we'd put the paper "to bed."

—Kathleen Donnelly

I had only visited The Squirrel Cage a few times before I reconnected with a longtime peripheral acquaintance and crash one night in a booth—a winter night in 2012, I believe. The relationship only lasted one-and-a-half years, but one of many things she turned me on to, was The Squirrel Cage cheeseburger that I still enjoy as often as I can. Delicious! Also, from the daytime lady to Billy and the crew at night, the staff is the best!

—Trym Killi

A good way to describe The Cage is good food, good company, and comfortable surroundings. I've been going to the Squirrel Hill Cafe since I started working at the J.C.C. (Jewish Community Center) in the late 1980s. I always have a good meal and great conversations with all of the regulars.

—Sharyn Stein

The Squirrel Hill Cafe, or The Cage, is one of the all-time Pittsburgh neighborhood bar icons. Good food, friendly atmosphere, and drinks served by men and women that are beyond compare. I've had some of the best conversations of my life with the employees and regulars at this establishment. I look forward to what comes next.

—Nick

I work at the JCC and always enjoyed the grilled provolone on sour dough bread. Best ever!

—Nancy Bell

I work right across the street from The Cage at Berkshire Hathaway Home Services. I have, for years, been coming over for their delicious burgers at incredibly reasonable prices. I love how unpretentious the bar is. When I have clients in from out of town, I love to bring them in for a beer and burger. Jan always takes great care and I always feel welcome.

—Bill Jacoby

I've worked at the library across the street. I've eaten from the cafe many times. I've enjoyed all that and have gotten my mom and other relatives to try the Cafe and they had good things to say about the food and service. I would strongly advise people to come to your place.

—Carmen

Squirrel Cage: At the time, a bar that was ahead of its time by W.D. Chrisner, III. Although I have no direct knowledge of this accomplishment, I believe that it is a story that must be told and celebrated. At some point the late 1950's or the early 1960's, The Squirrel Cage was one of the first places of public accommodation that made an effort to be accessible to individuals with disabilities, particularly those who used wheelchairs.

This story was told to me by my boss, Mr. Robert Pollock. We worked for a place called "The Home For Crippled Children" at the time I started there in December, 1971. The organization has changed its name since then and is now known as The Children's Institute.Back then, The Children's institute was a school, as well as residential rehabilitation/hospital facility for children and young adults, who were into their late twenties. Several of these young adults, particularly the guys, much like their peers without disabilities, wanted to get a drink at the local watering hole.

When they went to Squirrel Hill to do this, there weren't many options. The Squirrel Cage was receptive, but there were a couple steps to climb in order to get in the bar. In those days, there was no Americans with Disabilities Act (ADA). There was no local, State, or Federal requirement or Statute that encouraged or required places of public accommodation to welcome and serve people with disabilities. Therefore, the fact that the Squirrel Cage made the decision to remove the steps and replace them with an internal ramp was remarkable.

The Squirrel Cage was the first place that I know of that made such an extraordinary effort to accommodate individuals with disabilities. In my mind, this is what makes The Squirrel Cage such a warm, friendly, and welcoming water hole, and why it has been so enduring. Thanks so much for doing this and letting me tell this story.

—W.D. (Bill) Chrisner

I work right across the street from The Cage at Berkshire Hathaway Home Services. I have, for years, been coming over for their delicious burgers at incredibly reasonable prices. I love how unpretentious the bar is. When I have clients in from out of town, I love to bring them in for a beer and burger. Jan always takes great care and I always feel welcome.

—Bill Jacoby

I am from Toronto and used to visit my grandparents in Pittsburgh each summer. We started a tradition back in July of 1996, that when my grandma would play Mahjong, my grandfaher would take me to The Cage for a burger and he would drink an IC Light, and not tell my grandma. It's a great memory for me, and when I moved to Pittsburgh 20 years later, I still love this place.

—Ryan Muchmaker

I've been drinking and eating here for 35 years. Jan and I have become great friends over the years. Ronnie and I became good friends. Great food.

—Bob Parous

(R.I.P., July 15, 2018)

May 19, 2018, HANGING WITH THE GROWNUPS

In 1982, I was sixteen years old. I had spent the day in Squirrel Hill in the company of Ira and Jane, both of whom were social workers at the Jewish Community Center, and a couple of older teens. It had been a good day and I was happy to be included in a group of older folks. It was decided that all of us should go to the Squirrel Cage and hang out. Drinking did not even cross my mind, and even if it had, I am sure that nobody would have served me anything but a Coke. I just wanted to be part of this older, worldly crowd. I was psyched until Jan spoke up. "I don't think that a bar is the place for Annie," she determined. And so her word was law. I may have been young and sweet, but I wanted to smack her for shutting me out. The others went to have a good time, and I returned to my high school existence, and my room with the stuffed animals on the bed. I am now middle aged, and I still rarely drink. I love the bar food at The Cage, so I drop in once in a while. Always, there is a sense of rebellion when I enter and take a seat. I have to remind myself that I am, in all senses of the word, adult. It makes me happy to be there.

—Anne Alter

I remember coming here with my ex-husband and friends, (now one has recently deceased). We would go to the Squirrel Hill Theater and watch Marx Brothers movies, then come to The Cage. We did not own a car so we depended on buses to take us back to our "Love Shack" on Melwood Ave. in Oakland. Such good times.

—Candy Fenger

I'm a newbie; third visit. But I always feel at home here. Clearly there is a long history I need to learn about. I look forward to reading the book! Brava!

—David Gotwald

My husband (Brian) and I (Kristen) recently moved here from Lauranie, WY. We lived with my boss for 5 weeks and were forced out to a bunch of "yuppie" bars with over-priced beers (and a very poor selection) and too many hipsters. When we had some free time, we ventured into the Squirrel Hill Cafe and fell in love! We split a burger (which was <u>amazing</u>!) and had some beers. Now we are in our own place in Greenfield and frequent the establishment often. It feels like home! Thanks for making us feel welcome in this GREAT city!

—Kristen and Brian Edwards

I had the best times in The Cage and was sad when Ron moved away. Ron made me feel so welcomed. I had the best conversations with him. The many lunches I had there were the best lunches ever. Had it with many friends and met a few new friends. Whether it was celebrating someone's birthday or a moment in someone's life, it was always at The Cage. Have so many fantastic memories that I will cherish for a lifetime. Jan put me in many good moods when I was having a bad day. Always good to talk to Jan.

—Nancy Weitzman

Pitt student here from 1991-2001. Ten years of philosophy—good times. Best wishes. Thanks for the memories!

—Doug Dean

Great to be back after 20 years. You look great!
—Craig C. Ranolli

So good to be back at The Cage. A true Pittsburgh classic!

—Pat Doyle

I grew up in Squirrel Hill (I am 29 years old now) and the first time I ever was in a bar without my parents was at The Cage when I was 14. I was a volunteer at The National Aviary and we all went to see the documentary Winged Migration at the Manor. Afterwards we came to The Cage for a beer (not for me) and a burger. It was a great burger—and still is—and a great first bar. I am still coming back 15 years later.

—Marston Leff

I've been coming to The Cage for 10 years! The first time I came in to buy a beer I was 20 years old and Bill carded me and I had to wait another year before I could really begin my patronage. A lot has changed in my life over the years but even now I have good memories, some pretty blurry, of friends and good times at The Cage. Even now, 10 years later, it feels good to have a neighborhood place where you can catch up with friends and feel like a part of the community. It's always nice to see Jan when I stop in for coffee. I'll keep stopping by as long as it's here. I hope that it stays open so the next group of twenty-somethings can enjoy the community and have the same experiences I had.

—Justin Lewis

Tony lived at home with his parents and I lived with my sister and her family. We started meeting at The Cage after work for 25-cent drafts and good food. The Cage is where we came to get to know each other and fall in love. 31 years later we are still married! Thank you Ronnie DeLallo!

—Nancy & Anthony Amberger

Not a story, just wanted to say thanks! This is the best bar! I never thought I'd be a regular at a bar. This bar holds a very special place in my heart. Thanks for being a part of something wonderful.

—Alexis Dyer

For a couple of years I was part of a steady group of guys and gals. Most nights we sat at the bar by the window, drinking, joking and carrying on. One midnight someone took a shot at us from across the street, probably with a pellet gun. Thank god for double windows. The outer one shattered but the inner one held. The next night we sat at the far end of the bar.

—The Dirty Poet

Before cell phones we watched "Squirrel Hill TV." The Cage was my regular stop on my way home when I worked downtown. A favorite pastime was to sit in one of the two or three chairs on the short end of the bar, turn around so our backs faced the bartender, sip on our beers and look out the big picture window that acted as a two-way mirror.

We would people watch: we could see them, but they couldn't see us. We watched people coming and going in the busy Forbes and Murray intersection and Dan Simon used to call it "watching Squirrel Hill TV."

—Larry Resick

About four years ago I started coming in and met Mano Mano—we're both philosophers—and became friends. We'd meet and discuss Plato while slowly getting blasted. The more we drank, the more lucid he became, while I had increasing difficulty focusing. I learned more about Plato—and life—from my favorite philosopher from Zimbabwe (Rhodesia) than I had in half a century solo! Mano Mano was truly a great man and friend. RIP.

—Anonymous

For the past five years, I've been eating at the Squirrel Hill Cafe. Upon arrival, I normally am greeted by a friendly waitress named Janis. I get my usual hamburger and chips. The establishment is location in the heart of Squirrel Hill. The mom-pop eatery is cozy and comfortable.

—Arthur Coley

My name is Tyrone Simmons. I've worked at Footers Cleaners for three years and I really enjoy Squirrel Hill Cafe. The food is really great and the people are really nice and I love it.

—Tyrone Simmons

Great burger and beer for under $12? Best deal in Squirrel Hill! Better than "gourmet" places like Burgatory for half the price!

—Chuck Franciscus

Squirrel Hill Cafe is a true testament to how accidents can lead to most memorable and fun nights. While walking the streets with friends, we decided to try this cafe at the ripe age of 21. Little did we know that night would lead me to forge great relationships while hearing the stories of unique Squirrel Hill locals. This place will always hold a special place, as the environment fosters true and special times!

—Evan L. Benza

I'd been at the Squirrel hill Cafe a few times around the end of college with some friends. Five or so years later, when I was looking for a place to read and drink a few beers during my days off, I remembered this place, and it just so happened that the conditions were perfect, exactly what I was looking for. Casual environment, and a light above each table ideal for reading.

—Kurt Brendel

It was always so cool to know there was another family as large as mine. Since we grew up with the DeLallos, we were treated like family by all, but especially Ronnie, with his big smile, and warm, kind eyes. What was really wonderful was when I came into his "Cage" he would greet me with a hug, introduce me to his buddies and often other of his family members would be here.

—Mary Devine

I came up one day to the Squirrel Hill Cafe after I moved back to Pittsburgh. I had argued with my husband, needed to have some quiet time and had heard about this place. To my surprise, the man behind the bar and the owner was Ronnie DeLallo—one of the people in a big family who went to St. Thomas for grade school. We were both happy to remember that connection and, when I told him why I was there, he brought me a beer and the whole day seemed better.—Joan Devine

The late 70s and early 80s, we used to come to the Squirrel Cage for the cheap beer and fun atmosphere. I later found out my husband also frequented this place but we did not meet for years to come.

—Susan Christy CMU '81

Shortly after moving here with my husband from Arizona, his MFA program people had a meet up at The Cage before school started.

The invite just said, "The Squirrel Cage" so we wandered all up and down Forbes, then Murray Ave, looking for it. We went into the Squirrel Hill Cafe to ask if they knew where this "Squirrel Cage" place was! That's how we found it. It's amazing that a place can be such an institution they don't even have to use their real name! I've been back many times since, and I'm so glad this friendly, underrated refuge is here!

—Jan McMillan

Whenever we come home to Pittsburgh where I was raised, we can't miss the Squirrel Hill Cafe. It reminds me of my youth in the South Hills of Pittsburgh 55 years ago! Since then, I've been to college in the Midwest war in Vietnam, and 40 years in professional life in California. I have been here for many happy occasions such as reunions, family gatherings, and birthdays. I've even been here for funerals and rough times in my personal life, but no matter what I have always found the food and atmosphere of this cafe very comforting.

—David A. Linn

In the 70s & early 60s city workers and steelworkers could cash their paychecks at The Cage. The food and drinks were reasonable and good

—William G Miller ("Cuddles")

One for the Ditch.
Born and raised in the Burgh, Squirrel Hill has always been an unsuspecting favorite of mine. Having moved away from home more than 30 years ago, the "cafe" is a symbol of good people and good times. This bar is a consistent reminder that local traditions are pervasive… and generally, the best.

Around the fine age of 24, a dear friend of mine sent me on a blind date with (get ready for this) her uncle's college roommate and best bud. I arrived at the Tavern on the Square skeptical at best, but came home confidently gushing to my mother that I was going to marry the man I met that night. Eight months later that proclamation would prove to be true: I was engaged to my blind date from Chicago, Ted. Soon, to this day, we'd be Ted and Peg.

Celebrating one night with the old North Hills gang, we arrived at a point in the night when most should go home. The uncle responsible for introducing us encouraged "one last stop." "One for the ditch!" I said with a grin, my all too familiar tagline that could only mean one thing and one place. Almost at the same time and nearly involuntarily, the two of us knew exactly where we should go: The Squirrel Hill Cafe.

This is also the moment I probably knew these people were going to be my family for life. Knowing full well that I was soon to move to Chicago, I sat in the very barstool I write this in today and captured the moment in my mind. It was comforting, but special, and still I knew it wouldn't be the last. Funny enough, here in 2017, rock star—legend bartender Jan asked me if I had a memory to share about Squirrel Hill. "One for the ditch!" I instantly replied as reflexive as a night 30 years ago with my friends and fiancé, now husband who sat beside me. "LOL mom, that's like your battle cry," my daughter said, sitting next to us, here on a visit for a wedding. And she's right—no matter where I am, there will always be a little smirk on my face when I open the last beer for the night. "One for the ditch" will always be a salute to the original crew night after night at my favorite hometown hole in the wall. Only made better by the fact that it's still around to share the tradition with my kids. Cheers.

—Peg Koch

The best thing Christopher ever did was introduce me to the Squirrel Hill Cafe.

—Corey McCombs

I didn't meet Stephanie at the Cage. We first met at a far less impressive establishment called the Rock Room, where after a long night of conversation, she tricked me into her car, then drove like a bat out of hell halfway across the city. That was nearly a decade ago and ever since we haven't been able to stay away from each other, although I'm proud that's more on me for picking up the slack than anything else.

Where she drove us to was Squirrel Hill and shortly thereafter the Cage became our #1 place to meet for drinks, food, revelry—and romance. There were many evenings where after a long day of work I'd stroll in, meet milady, and drink up until last call in a cascade of compelling arguments, laughter, friends, and lively conversation. Truly these were some of the best evenings of my life and I'll always look back on them knowing that at least for a while I lived up to carpe diem. These are not, however, what makes this place so special to us, they are only the foundation.

Trying to distill Stephanie into a sentence, paragraph, or even with words can't be done competently (leastwise not by me) but suffice it to say that she's a private person. Beautiful, clever, composed—she's all of these things—all overshadowed by what many consider to be shyness. Really, the woman is complicated. Compelling, intriguing and complicated. That made the prospect of proposing to her complex indeed. I wracked my brain for when and where and how to pop the question, a scenario where we could treasure the moment.

I must've only had the ring for a few days before I realized there was only one place we both really loved, somewhere that'll be here when we're older so we can revisit the site—The Cage. I remember it was windy that day and a cool summer night so she was wearing a hat (the hat phase went on for so long), the college crowd was light for the off-season session of classes, and all told, the business wasn't booming. Perfect conditions. We walked in and I gestured for us to sit in one of the open booths, third from the door and with me facing the entrance to make sure I didn't ask right when a friend was strolling inside.

At that point I was starting to lose my cool. Not my nerve—never my nerve. There's nothing about life I'm more sure about than Stephanie. I was getting anxious and though I'm extremely capable of maintaining my composure with most people, it's never held any water with her. She knew something was up. But she didn't know what.

We made small talk about the day and I drank her in. For people like me, there's only one moment like this in life. You only get one. There are feelings for other people, strong ones, but nothing as singular and attuning like the love I'm talking about. Everything was just right. The room was warm with a comfortable breeze flowing in and out, the bar was lightly crowded with the din of revelry, the light hit her beautiful face like the movie star she is.

Reaching out under the table I grasped her hand. She looked at me lovingly, coyly—our little secret in the room, just the way she likes. With my other I reached into my pocket and produced the box. We stared at each other in silence for a few seconds and then I put it into her hand and said, "marry me."

For the briefest moment confusion flashed across her eyes as she realized what it was, but only the briefest of moments. She didn't even look at the ring before replying and my heart soared. You see there were two things I was worried about with my proposal: firstly, that she is a classy lady used to life's finest, and secondly that she is extremely particular. This is why I told her instead of asking, but that's far and away the lesser reason.

She didn't look at the ring. My poor, bedraggled, homeless-looking self proposed to her in a bar—not even down on one knee—and she said yes without even looking at the ring.

That was half a decade ago now and every time we walk into the Cage or drive by, that's what I see: a shrine not just to revelry, camaraderie, or the city of my birth, but home to the first perfect moment in my life.

—Mike Myler

I first moved to Squirrel Hill in January of 1980. I lived at 5880 Darlington Road with Daphna Czernobiliski and Lawy (LE) McCullogh. Daphna and Lawy brought me to The Cage for the very first time the first week and I became a daily regular immediately. The friends that I made in those years of the 80s (Lawy Harman, Max Williams, SHAb and so many more) have remained my best friends almost 40 years later. I always loved the eclectic mix of wonderful people here, from CMU professionals to homeless philosophers, from biker carpenters to dancer waitresses. I've been gone from Pittsburgh and Squirrel Hill for 20 years more, but I always return to The Cage when I come home, and I always will.

—Chris Gendron

The Cage is a most wonderful place to come and enjoy yourself purely as yourself, with no reservations, no matter who you are. You'd be hard pressed not to run into old friends and make new alike, for The Cage is the definition of a community spot, and fosters a lively community itself. The bartenders are the friendliest in town, the selection and prices top-notch … if you're ever around, feeling lonely or down, The Cage will make you anew. This place is a definitive part of the Pittsburgh experience and we are all blessed to be a part of it.—Brennan Kaye

Having been a "legacy" here at The Cage for well over twenty-five years, one would imagine the memories would start pouring out. Shit, I agree. Thing is, when Jan asks you if you've written anything for her book yet and your response is, "Not yet, is that still a thing," clearly the pressure was enough to instill at least a bit of writer's block. Better yet, she handed me a single sheet of notebook paper and a pen!

I suppose Jan is probably one of, if not *the* earliest memory I have about this place. Remember when I mentioned that I've been a "legacy" for well cover twenty-five years? Well, I'm only thirty-three. Let that sink in for a moment.

Some people see Jan as a hard-ass and that certainly isn't

misconstrued. Doesn't take much to see she ain't putting up with your crap. Some people even think she's mean. Those people are blind. Maybe it's easy for me to see that she's a big softy though. Who else can say they remember sitting at the bar with their dad and his friends, having the best hamburger, and being asked if they wanted to watch "He-men" when they were six?

—Name Undecipherable

The Cage has been an establishment for those of us that work in the service industry. I worked at Gullifty's for almost 6 years and The Cage was a place for all of us servers to relax at the end of the night. We loved to come in and have a few beers and cigs to talk about our night.

Once Gullifty's closed, I began to visit The Cage during the day. That's when I discovered Jan and even some of our former customers. As I remained employed in the neighborhood, The Cage would often be just a place to grab a quick lunch, but the laughs and conversation can never be replaced.

—Sirvasha Evans

I have been living in Squirrel Hill for twenty years now, and the Squirrel Hill Cafe (a.k.a. The Cage) has been an institution of legendary status for all this time. It is the definition of a "neighborhood bar" in every sense of the word. Excellent atmosphere, fantastic staff, and the friendliest people I have ever met. If the cafe were ever to disappear, the loss to the neighborhood would be immeasurable. Thanks for all the good times!

—Sincerely, Craig S. Campbell

Going back to the mid 1980s, I remember working at the Squirrel Hill Newsstand. I remember Freddie coming in to play the lottery and talking sports. One of my best memories was my boss giving me one dollar and telling me to get a shot and a beer next door, (The Cage). I walk in and Freddie starts razzing me! Now anyone from Pittsburgh knows about an Imp and an Iron, so that's what I got, cost? One dollar exactly. So much fun going in and seeing people!

—Eric Rogalsky

"Cheers-esque" It may be a cliché, but afternoons are like Cheers. Everybody has a favorite seat, knows your name, has a primary story of who they are—it's comfortable and happy. The staff, especially Jan, are friendly, welcoming—confidantes. It's an oasis to me. The food is great, the people nice. I'm a day person, so don't know about the nights. It seems a different crowd. I really look forward to spending an afternoon—drinks, food, good music, and smiling faces—who wants more?

—Sue

Love The Cage! We (the staff at the dental office) come here for lunch at least once a week. We call Jan our lunch orders ahead of time and Jan is always accommodating and very nice. Food is reasonable and delicious, atmosphere is relaxing. Love Jan and The Cage.

—Loyal customers

Peculiar relationships are par for the course in a places such as this. A place non-smokers will congregate in spite of the risk and clothes that'll sometimes smell after a second wash. Camaraderie, drinks, food, the common commonality of drunks having it out however they do. People completing a routine. The usual.

The day shift stretches out mostly in silence but with TV being the strong exception. The bar is speckled with locals, some of whom have been walking through the door for over thirty years. We have a lot of those, and they mostly dress well.

The night shift brings on the younger crowd but not without their betters. The room gets loud and packed with all of them. Someone cranks the volume on the jukebox. Some folks are finding themselves, others are getting lost. The room is suddenly so smoky even the chain smokers need a break. Muddled in the frew there will be someone reading, someone writing, every day, every night. You'll see.

—Jesse "Yishai" Philip Wolfe

One summer evening, I and a couple staff at, what was then The Home for Crippled Children (now The Children's Institute), brought a patient to The Cage for his twenty-first birthday. Walter asked to celebrate this milestone at The Cage because he overheard staff talk about it before. Walter was fused at his hips and we helped him roll his prone cart all the way to The Cage.

Once we arrived, we stood him up at a table with the support of his leg braces. At least 20 people who knew Walter came to toast his twenty-first. Walter had a beautiful, strong spirit. He was born with spina bifida and at 21 years old only weighed eighty-five pounds. Walter competed in weight lifting tournaments around the east coast with his coach. Walter bench-pressed over three hundred pounds! We toasted Walter's twenty-first and his great spirit at the Squirrel

Hill Cafe that summer night as we toasted no other. Here's to Walter!

—Jeff Bisbee

I remember Squirrel Hill Cafe was our place to play. Some of my most memorable times were here! Growing up twenty years ago in the Cafe was a blast. The drugs were plentiful and so were the guys! In fact, I met my first husband here… I'm not sure if it was the Tussionex or the Quaaludes that attracted me to him. It could have been the music and smoke-filled room at The Cage. Whatever it was, it was a blast.

—Madeline Cleeite

New to the area for about two years and found what feels like home. The service is beyond amazing, the food is reasonably priced and tastes good, the atmosphere is welcoming. The minute you walk in the door, the staff welcomes you and the service is quick. Love coming here a few times a week to relax and enjoy the great service.

—Jeanette Sayesh

On a coldish, longish evening, shadows stretching past the walls, I walked in for my nightly with my brothers Arlo and Wyatt. As we sat trying to reconcile the day, well into our second pitcher (PBR—only the finest in punk rock hipster for our lips), we looked up as three proud, finest of the "master race" walked in, adorned with iron cross tattoos. Unarmed, we got ready to rumble. Billy (our second dearest tender, only to Jan), let his blue tipped e-cig hang loosely from his lips. He knew there was trouble a-brewin'.

We stood, slightly off balance ready to evict the troglodytes. Bill walks out from behind the bar, deftly halting our intentions for violence, asking the scum to leave. And that's the talk of how I almost got into a fight at The Cage for all the right reasons.

—Balser Carl Whitlatch III

As a Pitt student in the 80s, leaving Oakland and coming to Squirrel Hill was like having a mini-vacation adventure. And The Cage was the resort, filled with fun, comfort, hospitality and just a little danger. Thanks for many late-night getaways.

—Yours, Joe Kecskemethy

Coming to The Cage feels like coming to my living room, if my living room was welcoming and brilliantly dark. Somehow the bartenders understand my needs better than I do. It's basically the only reason I come to Squirrel Hill, except for slices and records. Where else can I get a burger and some sassiness for five bucks? The Cage doesn't ask much from you, but is able to provide solace and peace. Diversity and conversation go hand in hand here. This cafe offers the known and unknown in equal kind and I couldn't ask for more.

—Christopher Metz

1986-1973
The Squirrel Cage is where many of my memories started. Adventures fueled by underage drinking. The Cage was never a problem bar so we always felt safe here. It was also a plus that some of our professors drank here giving us access to information that was otherwise not available. My life was changed by my time here.

—Thank you (Anonymous)

When I was a kid in high school, I would walk by this place all the time. We always said Bill looked like Lynyrd Skynyrd. Not 6 years later he would become my main bartender through my early 20s. Bill was consistently fun to talk to. Same with Matt. Always down to talk about anything. It's a great place to relax.

When I first turned 21, I came here by myself. Eventually started coming as my main bar. The burger is what I always came for and the pitchers. Plus hockey was always on. I remember the whole 2016 Pens Stanley cup run I watched the games there. Grew my beard out. Became friends with some regulars. Even after that, I came here most of the summer following. There was also Halloween when I stopped by in a penguin costume and had a shot with some people. The Squirrel Cage is like the perfect time machine. See you guys soon. <3.

—James Volk

This place is special. I come when I don't want to feel, but I always end up feeling everything. I come when I want to feel and I end up loved. It is where I have learned the most about myself, sitting in my booth writing and reading. It heals: wounds you didn't even know you had through the nourishment of being SEEN. They see you here. It is a place to truly see yourself through the gift of food, drink, and non-judgment. The Cage is where you go to get free. Thank you all.

—Liana Maneese

I was a bartender at The Cage in the early 1980's. After my third day, money went missing from the register. The day's takings were robbed. They had the police interview me but Ronnie got a letter from the cook who moved to South Carolina. In the letter he admitted he stole the money. I kept working at the Cage for another year. Loved working here.

—Kieran Stenson,
Dublin, Ireland

The Cage is the bar where my parents had their first date. The Cage is in the neighborhood where I grew up. The Cage is the first place I came every time I arrived in Pittsburgh after I moved away. The Cage is the first place I came when I moved back to Pittsburgh for good. The Cage is the first place I think of when I want to bring my friends together. The age is my favorite bar in the world; the first in my heart.

—Nicholas Geremin Madonia

September 25, 1990, we walked into The Squirrel Cage—a couple of kids in Pitt grad school looking for a cold beer. The bar was packed. I walked over to the jukebox to play some music when a fellow student came up behind me. I said, "I love Steve Miller." He said, "Thank you." I looked at him wondering what he meant. He told me that was his name. I didn't believe him, so he showed me his ID. Turns out, that was his name. We spent the rest of the night talking. Eight years later, to the day, we got married. 29 years later, the beer is still cold and The Cage remains a special place in our hearts.

—Caralin Miller

Up street at The Squirrel Hill Cafe, A.K.A. The Squirrel Cage, everybody knows your name, your parents' names, your grandparents' names, and your great grandparents names. The old-fashioned, intentionally dimly-lit bar is known for its reasonably priced and absolutely delicious soups, sandwiches, and grilled food.

In the evening, everybody congregates at the bar to socialize with everyone they already know. The newfangled bar and restaurant on the avenue are right on the mark; but this old-fangled bar and restaurant is every bit, if not more, packed. May the Squirrel Cage and its customers survive many more generations. We appreciate you.

—Vicky L. Fuller

There is nothing like the warm embrace of an iconic bar… I lived many lifetimes here!

—Tanya Mendez

December 8, 2018 Saturday, sometime in the afternoon.

Fortuities! I have been in the Squirrel Cage off and on for the past 50, 60 years, and only today because there was a parking spot right in front.

Inside, at a booth, writing in my journal, I realized it was the same booth I sat with my mother and father when I was 13 or 14, in 1939 or 1940.

I lived with my parents, 2 brothers and 2 sisters at 5751 Bartlett Street for 25 years only selling the house and moving to St. Petersberg, Florida, in 1947 in hopes of protecting my father's life. He died in 1947.

I have lived all my life in Squirrel Hill with the exception of an eight-month stint at war's end in the military in Japan.

I was a teacher and football coach at Central Catholic High School for 35 years and live now, as a widower since 2015, at 6553 Dalzell Place for the past 60 years. The Cage is still home.

—Joe Scully

I moved to Pittsburgh in 2013 and started exploring the city. So many amazing places to experience, from museums to parks, historical landmarks to your favorite night life. I had started coming to Squirrel Hill in 2014 to get massages at Massage Envy Spa. I stumbled upon the Squirrel Hill Cafe probably in 2017 when I had some time to kill. It was like walking back in time. So many original things in this pub from the dumbwaiter behind the bar to original wood fixtures, etc. I walked in and met the most remarkable person, Jan. She greeted me with a smile and great conversation. I learned about the history of the bar and met so many regular patrons who have been coming here for years. This is a landmark to see. I have been coming there every couple weeks for years and still feel as welcome as the first day I came here.

—Al Berry

Jules and I met at The Cage one Saturday night in September 2005—my first time at The Cage, which I had trouble finding since back then, we didn't have Internet on our phones and it wasn't labeled "The Cage."

I was supposed to be on a date that night with Paul, a mutual friend who'd invited me to join him and his friends drinking in the crowded upstairs area at a long table. Among them was Jules, who had already spent many late evenings at The Cage himself, living only a few blocks away. It didn't take long before Jules and I began talking that first night, and we ended up leaving the bar together. When it was clear that we'd hit it off, Jules appeased Paul with several Bloody Marys the next morning (he was later in our wedding).

Without thinking much about it—it wasn't just that it was "where we'd met," there was something else about it—The Cage quickly became a fixture in our lives. As a central location, it marked everything both big and small. It was the first place and the last place we'd end up, no matter what else we had going on: we'd go to The Cage before going to a friend's house, we'd go there after work, we'd go watch a game, or go after a game (Super Bowl XLIII!). We'd go after a concert—or, if there wasn't a concert, Jules would just play the longest songs we could find on the jukebox (Sad-Eyed Lady of the Lowlands, Sister Ray, and Dark Star).

We'd be at the Cage the night before a big trip and again when we finally got home. We walked there in the snow—during Snowmageddon 2010—there wasn't much else to do! We rode there countless nights on our bikes, snow and all. In retrospect, perhaps we shouldn't have biked back home after all those pitchers (and Rusty Nails) but we were young and it was mostly downhill.

As the years have passed, all roads seem to lead back to The Cage for us. We celebrated our wedding there the night before we got married (young! We were just 24). When one of us had something to talk over, plan, or celebrate, we'd go there. Every birthday, every year, for 15 years—every anniversary for 12 years. When we had to put our family dog down, we went there to decompress and look at pictures of her. We saw many friends and family members through life's challenges, all from a Cage booth.

Our friends and colleagues from work and graduate school, many of whom were from out of town, met us at The Cage often, always at our suggestion. We even had our will written up there: when our friend Lynn was in law school he demonstrated proper process for writing a will on one of our napkins. With Christine as a witness and signatory we were assured that it was a valid document, but that Jules's clumsy wording could prove legally problematic.

When we first found out I was pregnant, we went to The Cage to eat veggie burgers and let the news sink in. Later, when I was far more pregnant, we would sneak into the Cage so I could eat a veggie burger with everything, Swiss, and fries (Jules gets the same, but without tomato) to satisfy my cravings for my favorite weekly meal since 2005. Tina and Christine would make sure we got our food quickly and kept me away from the smoke. In fact, I think Tina was the first non-family person we told our baby news to: she was suspicious when I didn't join Jules in a beer (I told them I'd been abstaining for nine long months). Sure enough, after our son Sebastian was born, we took him to meet The Cage crew. He even went trick or treating there in his very first Halloween costume (he was a tiger)! Since becoming parents, we still go to The Cage just about once a week. We meet there earlier in the day now, and usually have to call it quits after a beer or two, but it's still very much our home away from home.

—Lauren and Jules Krishnamurti

I have been coming here for years. It's a place I can relate to—homey, cheerful and a bar/restaurant—could I ask for more? Yes. Wonderful people. Those coming in, perching at the bar and those sitting a table or booth and those serving, the best. It's such a pleasant time. God bless you Cage and thank you!

—Jean Slesinger

RONALD J. DELALLO • BETHEL PARK

'Squirrel Cage' owner fed need for conviviality

BY JERRY VONDAS
TRIBUNE-REVIEW

Squirrel Hill has its own version of "Cheers" — a gathering place known for its food and hospitality.

For 30 years, Ronald J. DeLallo catered not only to the business community and the college crowds, but to the commuters who got off the buses at the corner of Forbes and Murray avenues.

Mr. DeLallo, of Bethel Park, owner of the Squirrel Hill Cafe, died of pancreatic cancer on Monday, May 17, 2004, at the Jefferson Regional Medical Center, Jefferson Hills. He was 52.

His business was commonly known as the "Squirrel Cage," a moniker given by the police officers on the beat because at one time it had steel bars on the front window.

Mr. DeLallo, who learned to cook when he was growing up, prepared what his customers considered the finest Italian wedding soup in the city and the tastiest ribs.

"There were 11 kids in our family who were supposed to show up for dinner," said his brother, John DeLallo Jr. "And if you weren't there on time, you made your own meal. Ron, who was always up to something, was seldom on time. He made many, many meals for himself."

Mr. DeLallo, who was raised in Bethel Park, was the son of John DeLallo Sr. and the late Ruth Felsinger DeLallo. His father for years operated an insurance agency and a public accountant office before getting in the restaurant business.

In 1969, following graduation from Bethel Park High School, Mr. DeLallo went to work for Ryan Homes as a carpenter.

Ronald J. DeLallo

Convinced that carpentry wasn't for him, Mr. DeLallo accepted his father's offer to run the Squirrel Hill Cafe, which the elder DeLallo purchased in 1974.

"Ron had the personality to operate a restaurant, and my father knew it," his brother said. "Ron was the kind of guy that could light up a room as soon as he walked in. He had an incredible wit and a great sense of humor, but was terribly opinionated. He didn't mind letting you know what he stood for or how he felt."

Restaurant manager Jan Cavrak, who worked with Mr. DeLallo for 23 years, said: 'Ron had an aura about him. I knew it the day I applied for a waitress job. And although we fought like a married couple, Ron forgot about it at the end of the day.

"Ron was a hard worker. His day began at 6 a.m. when he'd come in and start preparing the menu for the day."

Bill Nagel, the evening bartender, described his 18-year association with Mr. DeLallo as friendly and challenging. "Ron was quite a character and had a terrific sense of humor. He was straightforward and let you know how he felt."

Mr. DeLallo had purchased a home in Arizona — where he planned to go after he sold the business and retired — but he never got the opportunity to live there.

Mr. DeLallo is survived by a son, Ronnie Kitchen, of North Carolina; his father, John DeLallo Sr., of Mt. Lebanon; and 10 siblings: John Jr. and his wife, Kathy, of Johnstown, Cambria County, Raymond and his wife, Nancy, of Castle Shannon, Mary Ruth Buckholz and her husband, Tim, of North Carolina, James, of Vermont, David and his wife, Alicia, of Peters, Christine DeLallo, of Boston, Thomas and his wife, Tracy, of Imperial, Theresa Karl and her husband, Mark, of Connecticut, Bernadette Anderson, of Minneapolis, and Denise Thompson and her husband, Ted, of Georgia.

Friends will be received from 2 to 4 and 7 to 9 p.m. today at Freyvogel-Slater Funeral Directors, 112 Fort Couch Road, Bethel Park. A funeral Mass will be offered at 11:30 a.m. Friday in St. Thomas More Church, Bethel Park. Interment will be in Queen of Heaven Cemetery, Peters.

RIP—A Tribute to Squirrel Cage Regulars Who Have Passed

As noted, 40 years is a long time to be in one place and Jan has seen a lot of people come—and go, most notably Ronnie, the previous owner of The Cage. This chapter is a nod and a hug to all of those who have (and continue to) make The Cage a community of members and memories.

We apologize that we only have first names of most, but most likely, you know who they are.

Al Capello
Bev Russell
Bob Pauros
Brian King
Buddy
Coleman
Coral
Coke
Danny Morrow
Dennis
Ethan
Franklin
Freddie (Cook)
J.C.
Jeff
Jim (Cook)
John F. DeLallo, Sr.
John Gardman
John Slack
Lamont
Mano Mano
Mark
Maureen
Meyer
Mike Ketter
Murray
Ned Thorton
Ronnie DeLallo
Ruthie
Scratch
Shug
Tex

SLACK
JOHN ROBERT

Age 67, of Edgewood, PA, passed away Saturday, February 17, 2018, after a courageous battle with Esophageal Cancer. Born November 1, 1950, in Pittsburgh, PA, John graduated from Edgewood High School in 1968 and obtained a BA in Professional and Creative Writing from Carnegie Mellon University. Son of the late Robert and Jeanne Slack; John is survived by his sister, Carolyn Petrovic (Jim); brother, Tom Slack (Kelly); nephews, Greg and Chris Petrovic; and niece, Selena Slack. John was a free spirit who had a passion for music, writing, and deep philosophical beliefs. Growing up inspired by his favorite band, The Rascals, John played Hammond organ, sang in many bands, and composed and performed his original songs. He used his writing skills to produce scripts for film, and his natural talent for acting to appear in scenes for local Hollywood productions. A true sports fan, John never lacked opinion on the managers of Pittsburgh teams. He will be remembered as an engaging personality with a sharp wit, a brilliant sense of humor, and the ability to charm everyone he met. The family plans to honor John with a celebration of his life; details will be posted to Facebook soon.

DeLALLO
JOHN F., SR.

Age 85, of Bethel Park, on Tuesday, January 30, 2007. Beloved husband of the late Ruth H. DeLallo; loving father of John F. (Kathy) DeLallo, Jr., Raymond (Nancy) DeLallo, Mary Ruth (Tim) Buckholz, James DeLallo, David (Alicia) DeLallo, Christine DeLallo, Thomas (Tracy) DeLallo, Theresa (Mark) Karl, Bernadette DeLallo (Leland Anderson), Denise (Ted) Thompson and the late Ronald DeLallo; brother of Victorina Dieter and the late Edmund, Albert, George and David; also survived by 16 grandchildren and 7 great-grandchildren. Mr. DeLallo served in the Army Air Corps in Europe during WWII, received his Bachelor's Degree from Duquesne University and worked as an Accountant, Insurance Broker and Restaurateur. Funeral arrangements by **BEINHAUERS.** Friends welcome at 2828 Washington Road, Peters Twp., 724-941-3211 on Thursday and Friday from 2-4 and 7-9pm. A Mass of Christian Burial will be celebrated on Saturday at 11:30am in St. Thomas More Church. Interment Queen of Heaven Cemetery. Memorial contributions may be made to The Little Sisters of the Poor, 1028 Benton Ave., Pittsburgh, PA 15212.

Ned Thornton
March 26, 1956 - July 30, 2001

STANG
ETHAN M.

On Thursday, August 4, 2005. Beloved husband of Fredda Levy Stang; beloved father of William L. (Margie) Stang, Robert D. Stang and Lisa A. (Morton) Goldman; grandfather of Alison, Emily & Daniel Stang, Michael, Molly & Samuel Goldman. Mr. Stang was a graduate of the United States Navy School of Music and served in the United States Navy during WWII. He auditioned for Fritz Reiner, conductor of the Pittsburgh Symphony Orchestra, and was hired for the principle piccolo position. He was with the orchestra for 45 years. He was a member of the Music Faculty at Carnegie Mellon University, Carlow College and Chatham College. Services at **RALPH SCHUGAR CHAPEL, INC.** 5509 Centre Ave., Shadyside, on Sunday at 11 am. Visitation 1 hr. prior to services, (10-11 am). Interment Temple Sinai Memorial Park. Contributions may be made to Temple Sinai Fund for the Future, 5505 Forbes Avenue, Pittsburgh, PA 15217 or Pittsburgh Symphony, 600 Penn Avenue, Pittsburgh, PA 15222-3259.

KETTER MICHAEL L.

On Sunday, May 17, 2009, Michael L. Ketter, 48, of Pittsburgh. Beloved husband of Gina (Pitta) Ketter. Son of the late Robert Ketter and Lorelei Ketter. Brother of Kay Nottis, Sue White and Mary Ketter-Franklin. Daddy of Merlin, Zoron, and Putt-Putt. Michael was a much-loved Program Director and on-air radio personality with WBCQ international short-wave radio station. In the 1990s he was Operations Manager and on-air broadcaster for WYEP-FM. Michael was a professional photographer as well as composer of electronic music. No visitation. Private services to be held in western New York. Family suggests memorial contributions to Forbes Hospice, 115 S. Neville Street, Pittsburgh, PA 15213. Arrangements by STATHERS FUNERAL AND CREMATION SERVICES INC., 7400 Irvine Street, Pittsburgh, PA 15218, 412-271-7030. (www.stathersfuneral.com)
Send condolences at post-gazette.com/gb

MURRAY CREWE | Died Feb. 11, 2017

PSO trombonist's motto: 'Eat, drink and be Murray'

By Molly Born
Pittsburgh Post-Gazette

Long before he joined the Pittsburgh Symphony Orchestra, trombonist Murray Crewe showed up for one of his first U.S. auditions with only a mouthpiece.

As the story goes, the airline had lost his trombone, so he cobbled one together with borrowed slides and bell sections from musicians also vying for a spot in the Utah Symphony. After the final round, his own instrument appeared, and he asked for one more chance to play for the judges.

"The committee said, 'It doesn't matter. You won,'" recalled Jim Nova, a PSO trombonist. "He won the audition on somebody else's equipment. That's unheard of."

This instance of turning calamity into opportunity with plenty of flair was befitting of Mr. Crewe's credo: "Eat, drink and be Murray." Mr. Crewe, the former PSO principal bass trombonist whose vibrant personality he also brought to Duquesne University and Carnegie Mellon University as a music professor, died Feb. 11 of liver and kidney failure. He was 56.

Fellow musicians called Mr. Crewe a bass trombone legend known for his full, resonant notes that never sounded too strident, and for his ability to play delicate passages with skillful restraint.

"For me, Murray's playing was very elemental, organic. He's a real force of nature," said Peter Sullivan, principal trombone of the PSO, who played with him here for 17 years and in some concerts in Canada before that. "His approach was very operatic — his soft, expressive playing was as convincing as his signature fortissimo sound."

Mr. Crewe was the first Canadian trombonist to win a job in an American orchestra (Utah) and among the PSO's most "colorful characters," said Craig Knox, principal tuba of the PSO. And Rebecca Cherian, the orchestra's co-principal trombonist, said 15 years playing alongside Mr. Crewe, Mr. Sullivan and Mr. Knox were "the most gratifying musically and personally I could ever hope for."

Murray Crewe

Born in Regina, Saskatchewan, into a family of musicians, Mr. Crewe moved around Canada often as a child. He started playing in the high school band, first tuba, then, encouraged by a mentor, the bass trombone.

He attended the University of British Columbia, where he would meet his future wife, Linda, a fellow music major, then studied music with some members of the Chicago Symphony Orchestra brass section. He won principal bass trombone of the Quebec Symphony, and after stints in Salt Lake City and Toronto, landed in Pittsburgh in 1993.

In addition to playing in the PSO for 23 years and teaching music, Mr. Crewe recorded numerous brass albums and taught at festivals across North America. The Canadian Broadcasting Corporation even ran tribute programming in his memory on nationwide radio, Mr. Knox said.

Beyond Heinz Hall, Mr. Crewe was a sports fan, especially hockey. His son, Ralph, recalled June 12, 2009, when his father was playing Mahler's Symphony No. 2 "Resurrection" on the same night as Game 7 of the Stanley Cup Final. The moment the concert ended, the two ran across the street to watch the Penguins victory together.

"It was one of the most emotional days of my life," his son said.

In addition to his son and wife, Mr. Crewe is survived by a daughter, Emilie of Vancouver, British Columbia; a sister, Jenny Mitchell of Vancouver Island, British Columbia; and a brother, Bill Crewe of Memphis, Tenn.

The family has requested that people should attend concerts or other cultural events. A memorial likely will he held in April.

Molly Born: mborn@post-gazette.com or 412-263-1944.

Daniel Hibbs Morrow, Ph.D., October 2, 1949 –May 20, 2018

Dr. Daniel Hibbs Morrow served as a program evaluator and grants manager, with a specialization in education, analyzing assessment data to inform classroom instruction. He was deeply committed to improving educational standards and was an advocate for social justice. He co-founded and served as Executive Director for HEArt—Human Equity through Art—the nation's premiere journal of art and literature dedicated to fighting discrimination and promoting social justice, from 1996-2002. He served as the journal's on-line Fiction Editor from 2013-2016. Mr. Morrow was a collector of art and literature and a passionate gardener. He was a profoundly sensitive and intelligent writer, with a signature voice and legacy. Dr. Morrow is survived by his sister, Ellen Haynes, and brother, David Morrow. A memorial service will be held later in the summer to celebrate Daniel's unique and unflinching contributions to the world, his work and his belief in art as a vehicle for social change.

PAROUS
ROBERT, Sr.

Age 58, of Greenfield, passed after a short illness on Sunday, July 15, 2018. Preceded in death by his father, George Parous; survived by his loving mother, Shirley; loving father of Bob Jr. and Michelle; grandfather of Eva and Lucia; also survived by his siblings Karen (Ron) Tozzi, and George Parous; former husband of Tely. Friends will be received on Wednesday 2-4, and 6-8 p.m. in the **EDWARD P. KANAI FUNERAL HOME,** 500 Greenfield Ave. Funeral Thursday at 11:00 a.m. in the Funeral Home. In lieu of flowers, donations to the family may be made.

Retire?

"Time to hang up my apron? When people ask me when I will retire, my answer is I like having a full tank of gas in my car, so no, I am not ready to give up my second skin. You know, you have to pay to play."

What this means is that if you should happen to read this book and it encourages you to come for a visit—find your new home—Jan will probably greet you, provided you get there before 6 pm. That's something to look forward to.

Her final words of advice: "Guys, if you are sitting at the bar, make sure your shirt is tucked. No one sitting behind you at a table or a booth wants to see the crack of your ass.

"Everyone has a story. We hope you enjoyed ours."

Thanks To You

We would like to take a moment to thank many of the people who are a part of everyday Cage life—helping it run and thrive—as well as simply being a part of its overall character. These people may or may not have provided a "Page in the Cage" but we are sure they have their own place here.

- Al—Plumber
- Deann & Paul Fountain Products
- Vecinies Distributing Co.—Ryan
- Galli Beer Corp.
- Brentwood Distributing—Paul, Alex & Casey
- Pete—window washer
- United Vending (pinball & jukebox)
- Breadworks
- Reinhart—Food Distributor
- Jay—Bartender at the old Silkie's; works in Bloomfield now
- Lou Werner—Mailman
- Mark at the Murray Ave. Grill
- Ray, the exterminator guy
- Wubby
- Eshi
- Stewart
- Eli
- Slim
- Bernie
- Sally Stein—best friend
- Shawn (my big "Teddy Bear", who cleans the grease traps/hood of the stove

If we forgot anyone, we apologize and please know that after 40 years, it is hard to keep everyone where they belong, here in my heart.

—***Jan***

Cage Time:

Since Jan and I started working on the book in 2017, a number of notable changes have occurred. Most remarkably, Billy cut his beard! He always said he wasn't cutting it until he was out of debt; make of it what you will.

Carley, Ethan and Kira are no longer with us, Alex has become the night kitchen manager, Ariel joined the waitressing crew and Lamar is the new day cook. The outside facade was meticulously refurbished/restored for a fresh, authentic look and well, I kind of quit smoking (Leslie).

And, the book, it was finished during the Covid pandemic—the first time in nearly 100 years that The Cage was closed for any length of time. Jan & I no longer meet on Mondays. Instead, we leave notes for each other in my mailbox and talk on the phone. We're looking forward to the day when we can walk through that red door and, once again, go home.

Finaly from Jan & I, hearts with the Black Lives Matter movement. Peace. Justice. Equity.

Jan Cavrak is a Pittsburgh native who grew up in the east end of the city and raised her family here. Her daughter Amy, son-in-law Howard and grandson Alex live in the South Hills while her son Larry, his wife Suzanne and their sons Nicholas, Matthew and Andrew live in Maryland. Jan has worked as a server (waitress and bartender) at The Squirrel Hill Cafe since 1980. She makes a home with Bill Chaffey in Swissvale, where she grew up. Today, Jan spends much of her off time enjoying her cabin in Bedford and with her family and friends (especially Sandy). She loves music, roadtrips and an occasional sweet. Jan plans on working at The Cage until she drops there.

Leslie Anne Mcilroy won the 1997 Slipstream Poetry Chapbook Prize for *Gravel*, the 2001 Word Press Poetry Prize for her full-length collection *Rare Space* and the 1997 Chicago Literary Awards. Her second book, *Liquid Like This,* was published by Word Press in 2008 and *Slag* by Main Street Rag Publishing Company as runner-up to their 2014 Poetry Book Prize. Leslie's poems appear in *Grist, Jubilat, The Mississippi Review, PANK, Pearl, Poetry Magazine, the New Ohio Review* and more. She won the 2018 Gemini Flash Fiction contest for her piece, "The Old Point." Leslie was co-founder of HEArt—Human Equity through Art—and works as a copywriter in Pittsburgh, PA where she lives with her son Silas.